WRITTEN COMPOSITION INTERESTS OF JUNIOR AND SENIOR HIGH SCHOOL PUPILS

By
J. H. COLEMAN, Ph.D.

TEACHERS COLLEGE, COLUMBIA UNIVERSITY
CONTRIBUTIONS TO EDUCATION, No. 494

BUREAU OF PUBLICATIONS
Teachers College, Columbia University
NEW YORK CITY
1931

Copyright, 1931, by Teachers College, Columbia University

PRINTED IN
THE UNITED STATES OF AMERICA

THE RUMFORD PRESS
CONCORD, N. H.

ACKNOWLEDGMENTS

This investigation was made possible by the kind cooperation of many people, to whom I wish to acknowledge my debt of gratitude. To my dissertation committee—Professor P. M. Symonds, Professor E. K. Fretwell, and Professor Allan Abbott—I express my appreciation for their interest and counsel. To Dr. Symonds I owe a special debt for his constant help and inspiration.

I wish to thank Miss Jean Fraser of White Plains, Mr. Ellis H. Drake of Kalamazoo, Mr. J. E. Hughes of Stamford, Mr. Hubert Mott of Seneca Falls, and Mr. R. K. Toaz of Huntington for extending the facilities of their schools and for securing the cooperation of their teachers for this work. I am particularly happy to thank two of my former teachers, Miss Sarah Elder and Mr. C. C. Wilcox, for carrying out the work in Kalamazoo.

To Miss Marjorie Chase I extend my thanks for reading portions of the manuscript and for assisting with the clerical details. Finally, I wish to acknowledge my appreciation to my wife, Louise H. Coleman, for her help with much of the clerical work and for her constant encouragement.

J. H. C.

CONTENTS

CHAPTER	PAGE
I. Statement of the Problem	1
II. Plan of the Inquiry	6
III. Interests Indicated by the Titles of Free Choice Compositions	16
IV. Written Composition Interests Indicated by Pupils' Choices from Lists of Titles	26
V. Pupils' Reasons for Choosing Specific Titles	63
VI. Written Discourse Preferences of Secondary School Pupils	70
VII. Review of Conclusions, with Recommendations for Their Use	84

APPENDIX

I. Directions for Ranking These Lists of Titles	89
II. Composition Investigation	99
III. Samples of Types of Discourse Questionnaires	104
IV. Unclassified Free Choice Composition Titles	108
V. Unclassified Reasons Which Pupils Gave for Choosing Specific Topics	112

TABLES

NUMBER		PAGE
I.	Definitions of Categories of Interests Represented by Composition Titles	9
II.	Titles Selected for A, B, and C Lists	10
III.	Total Number of Returns on Composition Title Preferences for Each Grade	14
IV.	Approximate Number of Pupils Who Used Lists of Titles	15
V.	Total Number of Pupils Writing Free Choice Compositions	16
VI.	Rank Order List of Boys' Free Choice Composition Interests	18
VII.	Rank Order List of Girls' Free Choice Composition Interests	19
VIII.	Rank Order List of Boys' and Girls' Free Choice Composition Interests	20
IX.	Returns on Composition Title Preferences	27
X. to XXVII.	Rank Order Lists of Composition Title Ratings by Grades for Each Sex and for Both Sexes Combined	29–46
XXVIII.	Rank-Difference Coefficients of Correlation for the Three Possible Pairs of Combinations of the A, B, and C Lists	47
XXIX.	Correlations of the Rank Order Lists Between Grade Seven and Each of the Other Grades	48
XXX.	Categories of Interest Discarded Because of the Chance Character of the Data	49
XXXI.	Composition Topic Likes and Dislikes Common to All Grades for Boys and Girls Together	50
XXXII.	Composition Topic Likes and Dislikes Common to Boys in All Grades	52
XXXIII.	Composition Topic Likes and Dislikes Common to Girls in All Grades	53
XXXIV.	Grade Lists of Composition Topic Interests Arranged by Sexes	56
XXXV.	Sex Preferences in Composition Topic Interests Common to All Grades	56
XXXVI.	Composition Topic Likes and Dislikes Common to Both Boys and Girls, with Medians	57

NUMBER		PAGE
XXXVII.	Rank Order Lists of Pupils' Reasons for Choosing Specific Topics	67
XXXVIII.	Rank Order Lists of Per Cents of Pupils Giving Particular Reasons for Choosing Specific Topics . . .	68
XXXIX.	Returns on the Types of Discourse Questionnaires . .	71
XL. to XLV.	Rank Order Lists of Written Discourse Preferences by Grades for Each Sex and for Both Sexes Combined .	72–78
XLVI.	Rank Order List of Types of Composition Preferences (by Type Number)	79

WRITTEN COMPOSITION INTERESTS
OF JUNIOR AND SENIOR HIGH
SCHOOL PUPILS

CHAPTER I

STATEMENT OF THE PROBLEM

The problems of this investigation center around the English composition interests of pupils of junior and senior high school grades. The chief concern was to determine some of the topics which pupils prefer to use as subjects for compositions and to learn which types of written discourse are preferred by pupils from the seventh grade through the twelfth grade. Specifically, the object was to find answers to the following questions: What topics do pupils prefer to write about? Which types of discourse do they like? Are there sex differences in these interests? If so, what are they? Do interests tend to vary among different grade groups? If so, what are the variations?

There is a condition today which makes these questions appropriate. The results of English composition teaching are generally unsatisfactory. There is dissatisfaction with the ability in written English of pupils who enter high school and of those who leave high school to go to institutions of higher learning. As a result, a multitude of efforts have been directed toward the improvement of written composition. These have dealt variously with curriculum phases of the problem, with the mechanics of written expression, with efforts to establish objective standards of ability by means of composition scales, and with different methods of composition teaching.[1]

The task of finding means for improving the quality of written compositions is decidedly difficult. Not only is composition writing itself a complex function, unwillingly lending itself to careful analysis, but the problem is further complicated by the demand to secure improvement for all the heterogeneous group of pupils now composing our high school population. Under these circumstances a greater use of the potentialities of interest commends itself.

In the literature of education, interest has become synonymous with concentrated attention, with persistency, with an attitude

[1] Lyman, R. L., *Summary of Investigations Relating to Grammar, Language and Composition*. Supplementary Educational Monographs, Number 36. University of Chicago, Chicago, Illinois, 1929.

which develops rapid learning. Interest provides zest and drive. It is an aid to that continuity of effort which is needed for the successful conclusion of a learning activity. It is satisfying to the learner. It is dynamic. Every unprecedented achievement in science, invention, or art bears witness to the unusual amount of labor and effort which interest engenders. There are those who contend that there is no real learning without genuine interest.[2] A lack of interest in written expression has its special importance. The mechanics of writing are so numerous and so involved, and the acquisition of style is so difficult, that they tend to discourage pupils at almost every step toward mastery. A dislike for composition is the most probable development. This dislike interferes with the mastery of any topics introduced later and contributes to the impermanence of items learned previously. For most pupils, every bit of drive which interest can muster is required for the attainment of desirable proficiency in written discourse.

Two factors of interest are important to the teacher who would capitalize the values to be derived from pupils' interests in written composition. The first is that "interest does not end simply in itself . . . but is embodied in an object of regard."[3] One is interested *in* something. Consequently, it is possible to list these objects of interest. The second factor, also, is stated by Dewey[4]: "things indifferent or even repulsive in themselves often become of interest because of assuming relationships and connections of which we were previously unaware." By our definition of genuine interest, this shift in interest depends upon an awareness in the pupil of the new relationships. An example will serve to make this clear. A pupil writing about his hobby has something to say. Any inadequacies of expression are barriers to making himself clear. There is an immediate need for improvement, an awareness of the relationship between the inadequately composed theme and the way

---

[2] For the sake of clarity, it is worth while to give a definition of genuine interest. In *Interest and Effort in Education*, Dewey distinguishes the "soft" from the "hard" pedagogy. The former attempts to make interesting some subject matter (disagreeable to the child) because it is felt he should master this particular activity. The latter makes the same assumption concerning subject matter but attempts to secure mastery by threats or punishment. Neither represents genuine interest. Intrinsic interest is apparent in activity originated by the child as part of his self-development. The purpose to do is his. The activity has value for itself, not for the avoidance of punishment or for the mere appearance of a value which does not exist.

[3] Dewey, John, *Interest and Effort in Education*, p. 16. Riverside Educational Monographs. Houghton Mifflin Company, Boston, 1913.

[4] *Ibid.*, p. 22.

to overcome this lack through improved technique. A genuine interest can be created in an activity deemed worth learning, when the activity can be related to the child's experience. To sum up, with a knowledge of pupils' interests in composition, it would be possible, and psychologically in keeping with the principles of genuine interest, to direct their energies toward specific improvement in written expression. Such a course of action is calculated to derive the most efficient and economical learning by securing interest.

Apparently, very little study has been directed toward pupils' interests in composition. In 1913, Harris [5] reported a study, the purpose of which was "to determine, if possible, the dominating lines of interest of the child with reference to the material for composition." The inquiry was begun in Minneapolis in 1910. One portion of the study was devoted to the types of discourse which pupils prefer to use. Two methods were employed. With each method, this question was presented to the pupils: "If you were asked to select a topic for written composition from one of the following kinds or types, which would you select as your first choice? Your second choice?" In the first instance, this statement was followed by four specific topics for each type of discourse; for example, "A reasoning topic, such as: Why United States senators should be elected by the people; why arithmetic is a more valuable study than history; why playgrounds should be established; some reasons why I desire an education." In the second case, in which the topics were shuffled when they were distributed, Harris merely stated the four types, as follows: a reasoning topic; an explanatory topic; a narrative topic; a descriptive topic. He secured a conclusive demonstration that narration and description are largely preferred in that order. Choices were made by 522 pupils.

The second part of his investigation was an attempt to rank eleven different topics on which pupils gave first, second, and third choices. He secured rankings from 520 pupils, and made up the list on the basis of the percentages of combined choices. The topics in the order of their preference were as follows: biography, history, manual training and cookery, personal actual experience, personal imaginary experience, other's imaginary experience, literature, other's actual experience, civil government, geography, and physi-

---

[5] Harris, J. H., "An Inquiry into the Composition Interests of the Pupils in Seventh and Eighth Grades." *English Journal*, Vol. II, pp. 34–43, January, 1913.

ology and hygiene. His conclusion from this study (p. 39) was that "enough has been shown, it seems to me, to indicate that the most effective method in compositional work is to allow considerable latitude of topic, and not, as is generally the case, to require pupils in a class or school to write on the same topic whether interested or not."

Three more studies of doubtful significance relate to pupils' interests in composition. Laidley [6] examined varying numbers of issues of forty-six junior high school publications in an effort to classify the articles into groups of interests. She found the largest number of articles written on the following seven groups: (1) general school news, (2) verse, (3) jokes and personals, (4) club news, (5) stories, (6) moralities (thrift, school spirit, etc.), and (7) informational essays. Concerning the four principal types of discourse, she found them combined most frequently. Description alone was practically never used, and narration consisted of a plain statement of facts. Exposition, sometimes coupled with persuasion, was most prominent. Webster and Smith [7] classified the compositions of 10,000 pupils in thirty junior high schools. Pupils selected their own topics, which were classified under five headings. These are given in the order of preference, the first being preferred more than all the others combined: (1) personal experience, (2) imaginative themes, (3) how to do or make things, (4) school expeditions and community enterprises, (5) current events or community problems.

Ballard [8] made a study of the prose preferences of 446 boys and girls between the ages of eight and fourteen. The pupils rated and criticized four versions of an extract from Sir Thomas Malory's *Morte d'Arthur*. Ballard found that children's tastes regarding the form of prose, distinct from the content, are not easy to ascertain, for the class tends to re-echo the judgments of the teacher. A fondness in children for a florid style of writing increases with age and reaches its maximum at about the middle of adolescence. The whimsical and humorous style in which many books for the young

---

[6] Laidley, Mary Fontaine, "Composition Interests of Junior High School Pupils." *English Journal*, Vol. XIV, pp. 201–09, March, 1925.

[7] Webster, E. H. and Smith, Dora V., "The Danger of Dogma Concerning Composition Content." *English Journal*, Vol. XV, pp. 414–25, June, 1926.

[8] Ballard, P. B., "Prose Preferences of School Children." *Journal of Educational Psychology*, Vol. V, pp. 10–21, January, 1914.

are written finds much favor with children up to about ten years of age, after which the tendency is to regard it as babyish.

These four references seem to constitute all the available studies of a reasonably objective nature which throw any light on pupils' interests in composition. They have served to guide portions of the present study, in which the aim was to secure a wider range of information.

CHAPTER II

PLAN OF THE INQUIRY

A. What Topics Do Pupils Like to Write About?

Two methods were employed in an effort to find an answer to this question. By the first method, pupils were asked to write a composition upon any topic of their own choosing. The titles of these compositions were classified according to certain broad definitions of interest described under the second method. Additional categories were made for titles which could not be classified according to the list used in the second method. It should be noted that these titles were chosen by the pupils under typical classroom conditions. Teachers were asked to substitute this free choice of topic composition for their own assignment.

By the second method, pupils were asked to write three compositions, using titles selected each time from a list handed to them. There were three lists: A, B, and C. Cooperating teachers were asked to use these lists instead of assigning topics for compositions. Since it is a common practice to assign one composition a week, it was suggested that the lists be used in that way. The one requirement was that each pupil should actually write a composition upon one of these titles. He was asked also to rank the titles which he liked next best, those which he liked least or disliked most, and those which he liked next least. By asking that a composition be actually written, it was expected (1) that a careful, not a perfunctory, choice would be made, and (2) that each title on the list would be examined by the pupil.

Thirty-six categories of interest were represented. In order to prepare this list, a study was made of researches in other fields of pupils' interests. On the assumption that pupils may like to write about the same general topics which are their preferences in reading, the studies of interests in reading by Jordan [1] and Washburne [2] were investigated.

---

[1] Jordan, Arthur M., *Children's Interests in Reading.* Contributions to Education, No. 107. Bureau of Publications, Teachers College, Columbia University, New York, 1921.

[2] Washburne, Carlton and Vogel, Mabel, *What Children Like to Read.* Rand McNally & Company, Chicago, 1926.

Jordan concludes (pp. 128–29): "That the major interests of boys from 10 to 13 years in reading are included in four general types of fiction: (*a*) Books concerned with war and scouting; (*b*) those concerned with school and sports; (*c*) those concerned with the Boy Scouts; and (*d*) those concerned with strenuous adventure. . . . That in non-fiction, the interest centers around what-and-how-to-do-books. . . . That the interest in biography and history is confined to those authors who can write biography and history in the form of an exciting story.

"That the interests of girls are concerned principally with fiction which portrays: (*a*) home; (*b*) home and school; (*c*) school; (*d*) fairy stories; (*e*) stories with historical background; (*f*) love; (*g*) miscellaneous.

"That except for a few books on cooking, crocheting, dramatics and poetry, girls fail to show interest in non-fiction." He also lists the chief satisfiers deduced from books frequently chosen for both boys and girls; these were suggestive of possible topics they might prefer to write about. For boys he gives this list of satisfiers:

"Physical strength and aptitude.
Self-control, particularly in critical situations.
Independence based on actuality.
Making the team at the expense of an unjust rival.
Saving a person's life.
Gaining the mastery in a physical combat when the opponent is despicable.
Being loyal.
Going somewhere.
Having new experiences of almost any kind.
Gaining the plaudits of his fellows.
Being honest, straightforward, open, trustworthy.
Winning admiration, even of an enemy, in these things."

Following is a list of satisfiers for girls:

"Kindliness to others, especially to those who are in distress.
To wear beautifully tailored clothes.
To hold her position socially as high as any one.
In being honorable and possessing a clean mind.
In unselfishness.
In playing pranks at school.
In being honest at school.
In gaining the esteem of those worth while at school.
In being loved and admired for oneself.
In protecting those weaker.

In having things happen.
In being open and not deceitful.
In getting a box from home, in having a feast till late hours, and in telling stories.
In success in dramatics.
In going to a city, if raised in the country."

The Winnetka Graded Book List does not differentiate for boys and girls, but gives the following lists of interests in reading:

"*Seventh Grade:* Adventure and chivalry, family life, winning prizes, dogs or animals, motherliness, good moral character, humor, love or romance, calling forth sympathy, getting rich, mysteries, Indians, fairyland, travel, school, patriotism, children, war heroes, biography.

"*Eighth Grade:* Danger, imaginative (books), teaching school, poetry, pirates, self-sacrifice, Indians and cowboys, biography."

Another source used as a guide in selecting a list of topics for compositions was the titles suggested in current textbooks in English composition. All of these available in the Textbook Library at Teachers College were searched for composition titles.

Studies of the interests of junior high and senior high school pupils in general science presented minor interests that could not be included in a study, such as the present one, that aimed to explore the larger fields of interest. It was sufficient for our purposes to use the entire field of science as one interest. This is true also of studies of pupils' likes and dislikes concerning various school subjects. Studies of the interests of elementary school children in reading and in art did not reveal any material which had not already been covered.

From all these sources, thirty-six categories of interest were eventually defined; these are given in Table I. The list is in no sense all-inclusive. Its categories are broadly defined. It is fairly comprehensive and offers ample opportunity for pupils to differentiate between interests. It is not too long for each pupil to peruse the entire list carefully if his assignment stipulates that a composition is to be written upon some one title appearing on the list.

In order to secure the most appropriate titles for each interest, a list of ten titles for each category was made out, to be submitted to qualified judges for ranking. Some of the titles were taken from texts; others were made for the occasion. In the opinion of this author, these titles were ten of the best available. Nine persons, either professors of secondary education, literature, or psychology, or teachers of English composition in secondary schools, were asked

TABLE I
DEFINITIONS OF CATEGORIES OF INTERESTS REPRESENTED BY COMPOSITION TITLES

1. Adult Occupations or Vocations: Occupations or vocations in which adults engage.
2. Adventure: In which danger, daring, mystery, or some other excitement is the central theme.
3. Animals: Any kind.
4. Art: Includes painting, freehand drawing, sculpture, design, etching, modeling, and wood- and linoleum-cutting.
5. Athletics and Sports: Includes all organized or team games.
6. Children: Those younger than the pupils using the title for a composition.
7. Civics: Problems of government.
8. Contemporaneous Famous People: Any living individual.
9. Current Events: Noteworthy happenings of the immediate present.
10. Ethics: Having to do with standards of conduct.
11. Fairy Tales and Legends: Any fairy tale or legend.
12. Getting Rich: Central theme concerned with having or obtaining wealth.
13. Handwork: The purpose of doing some piece of such work.
14. Health: Any phase of personal or public health or of physiology which the pupil may be familiar with.
15. Historic Events, Sites, or Characters.
16. Home Life or Participation Therein by the Pupil.
17. Humorous Anecdotes: Stories or incidents.
18. Indefinite Titles: No definite kind of composition is suggested by the title.
19. Leisure Activities: Any pleasurable activity of the pupils which is not classified elsewhere on the list.
20. Literature: Any feature of books, poetry, or literary article which pupils have read.
21. Machines: Description or qualities of the mechanism of any machine.
22. Modern Industries: Any phase of the process or physical equipment of any modern industry.
23. Music: Any phase.
24. Outdoor Activities: Any outdoor activities other than organized or team athletics.
25. People: Character studies or descriptions of appearance.
26. Personal Experience: In which the pupil talks about himself.
27. Proverbs.
28. Pupil Employment for Financial Remuneration: After-school jobs or other methods of earning money while attending school.
29. Religion: Church, religious organizations, Bible study, or Religious History.
30. School: Any phase, curricular or extra-curricular, where the central theme is the school.
31. Science: Anything included in classes in the school in General Science, or any phase of the specific Physical or Natural Science Courses.
32. Sentiment: Love for or interest in someone of the opposite sex.
33. Social Problems: Problems pertaining to society or its organization.
34. Sympathy: Sympathy or kindness toward some person or animal.
35. Travel: Places to visit or places visited.
36. Winning Prizes: Any phase of winning medals, letters, or other prizes.

TABLE II
Titles Selected for A, B, and C Lists
The Combined Values Assigned by Nine Judges to Each of Ten Titles Submitted for Each Category of Interest

Number Designating Each Interest	Number of Each of Ten Titles Submitted to Judges										Rank		
	1	2	3	4	5	6	7	8	9	10	First	Second	Third
1......	39	15	4	13	23	4	0	28	17	7	1	8	5
2......	10	26	26	8	10	12	30	0	9	19	7		2–3
3*.....	17	10	14	34	30	3	1	4	3	32	4	10	5
4......	22	9	23	2	22	0	6	33	0	33		8–10	3
5......	22	8	4	2	20	11	27	31	24	1	8	7	9
6......	21	18	3	20	1	13	13	9	22	30	10	9	1
7......	34	5	19	3	11	31	11	18	7	11	1	6	3
8......	25	4	20	29	24	43	0	3	2	0	6	4	1
9......	42	26	3	9	7	8	5	3	6	41	1	10	2
10.....	7	12	14	35	14	8	27	16	7	10	4	7	8
11.....	25	27	1	14	14	26	6	17	17	3	2	6	1
12.....	35	14	18	2	30	6	11	11	4	19	1	5	10
13.....	10	16	17	23	10	19	0	31	10	14	8	4	6
14.....	30	0	16	9	20	16	13	2	30	14		1–9	5
15.....	18	10	5	29	19	18	21	6	5	19	4		5–10
16.....	14	22	24	22	15	2	3	11	21	16	3		2– 4
17.....	31	8	27	1	2	19	4	31	0	27		1–8	3–10
18.....	40	22	13	12	15	6	12	23	7	0	1	8	2
19.....	31	29	15	9	17	0	0	19	18	12	1	2	8
20.....	29	6	20	9	3	10	16	21	9	27	1	10	8
21.....	14	16	0	19	4	46	27	1	12	11	6	7	4
22.....	37	32	23	31	1	2	7	2	10	5	1	2	4
23.....	36	4	10	15	15	3	17	25	9	16	1	8	7
24.....	35	26	10	0	9	30	0	19	19	2	1	6	2
25.....	29	22	11	20	7	3	3	11	26	18	1	9	2
26.....	13	20	8	30	9	9	22	5	15	19	4	7	2
27.....	14	26	20	11	14	16	32	8	5	4	7	2	3
28.....	30	18	14	0	13	13	23	18	2	19	1	7	10
29.....	7	26	14	10	23	13	8	13	29	7	9	2	5
30.....	8	30	24	9	20	0	20	23	1	15	2	3	8
31.....	9	28	16	5	23	6	4	25	15	19	2	8	5
32.....	10	18	16	13	9	3	22	23	31	5	9	8	7
33.....	7	6	18	28	18	24	20	4	17	8	4	6	7
34.....	19	15	11	22	9	20	10	21	15	8	4	8	6
35**....	41	5	0	8	0	0	28	12	36	17	1	9	7
36.....	29	17	24	4	4	24	11	30	3	4	8	1	3–6

*One ranker omitted one ranking.   **One ranker omitted two rankings.
Ranks were assigned values as follows: 1—5; 2—4; 3—3; 4—2; 5—1.

to rank the best five titles in order of merit according to the following conditions: (1) for the accuracy with which any given title is related to its category, as those categories are defined in Table I, and (2) for the suitability of any given title, in so far as the general topic is common experience for pupils of both sexes, ranging from the seventh grade to the twelfth grade. Complete instructions and lists of titles are given in Appendix I.

To tabulate these judgments, a ranking of 1 was credited with 5 points, 2 with 4, 3 with 3, 4 with 2, and 5 with 1. Table II shows the tabulation of these rankings, together with the three titles having the highest combined rankings. These three titles were selected for the lists from which the compositions were written. Three lists, A, B, and C, were made. The A list contained all the titles ranked highest in each category, B contained those ranked second, and C contained those ranked third. In cases of tied rankings, first choice was given to the title appearing first on the lists given to the judges.

To neutralize the effect of position on the lists, four different sets of each list were printed. In the first set all the titles were in correct numerical order; in the second set the first nine titles were shifted *en masse* to the bottom of the list. In the other two sets similar shifts were made so that the four different A lists had the following category numbers at the top: 1, 10, 19, 28. This secured a rotation in position for each block of nine titles, first at the top of the list, then at the bottom, then at the lower middle, and, last, at the upper middle position. Before the lists were sent out, they were arranged in this order with the result that, so far as the position of the titles was concerned, five papers had to be passed out in a class before one was duplicated. A copy of each of these three lists, in correct numerical order for list A and in shifted positions for lists B and C, is given in Appendix II.

B. Which Types of Discourse Do Pupils Prefer to Use for Written Composition?

The purpose of this inquiry was to determine the types of written discourse which pupils prefer to use when they are free to make their own choice. Harris, in the study previously referred to, felt that there was a "conclusive demonstration" that pupils of the seventh and eighth grades prefer the four standard types of written discourse in the following order:

1. narrative   2. descriptive   3. reasoning   4. explanatory

He adds that narration and description are mainly preferred.

In this study the list of types of discourse was extended to include ten different types commonly used in written composition classes. This list, together with designating numbers and definitions for each type, follows:

1. Narration   —Write a story.
2. Description   —Describe the appearance of something.
3. Exposition   —Explain why or how something happens.
4. Argument   —Give reasons for opinions or conditions.
5. Friendly letter—Write one.
6. Business letter—Write one.
7. Poetry   —Write a poem.
8. News article   —Write one suitable for a school paper.
9. Editorial   —Write an essay suitable for a school paper.
10. Debate brief —Write one for either side of a debate.

Interest in these types of written composition was surveyed by means of a questionnaire as part of the interest study in which teachers were asked to cooperate. A subject for the composition was proposed to pupils, and they were asked to indicate the type they preferred most, next most, least, and next least. In order to obtain answers as nearly as possible on the basis of type alone, four different subjects were chosen for four different sets of the questionnaire. The topics, in their order, were as follows:

Q1A. Winter   Q1B. Airplanes   Q1C. Games   Q1D. Movies

Copies of each of these questionnaires are to be found in Appendix III. As far as possible, the wording and the directions for each set were the same. To overcome advantages of position, every other paper in each group was printed with the last five types of discourse first. This arrangement is shown in the samples of Q1B and Q1D.

C. Schools Cooperating in the Study

For practical reasons the study was limited to pupils in each grade who were taking courses in written composition. This condition included practically every pupil in the grades where composition is a required subject. Three aims were kept in mind at the outset: (1) to secure the cooperation of cities that were representative, for the grades involved, of the United States; (2) to survey the entire school population in a community within the given grades; and (3) to secure approximately 1,000 pupils for each grade.

Plan of the Inquiry

It is recognized that high school populations today are selective so far as the total possible high school age population of the country is concerned. Therefore, the results of this study can be representative only of pupils in English courses in junior and senior high schools.

The following cities and villages cooperated:

> Huntington, N. Y.
> Kalamazoo, Mich.
> Seneca Falls, N. Y.
> Stamford, Conn.
> White Plains, N. Y.

The following descriptions of these cities are taken from the *Encyclopedia Americana* (copyright, 1924). The populations given are those of the United States Census for 1930, taken as of April 1.

Huntington, N. Y. Vol. 14.

Pop. (Huntington Town)—25,581. A town in Suffolk County on Long Island; on Long Island Sound and on the Long Island Railroad. From the first, agriculture was the chief occupation. Large market gardens are in parts of the town, but much of it is a favorite residential suburb of New York.

Kalamazoo, Mich. Vol. 16.

Pop. 54,786. Kalamazoo is in a rich agricultural region. Few cities of the United States of a corresponding population show such a diversity of industrial corporations. It has over 276 manufacturing establishments. Some of its prominent institutions are: Kalamazoo College, opened in 1855 under the auspices of the Baptist Church; Nazareth Academy, Roman Catholic; Western State Teachers College; Borgess and Bronson Hospitals.

Seneca Falls, N. Y. Vol. 24.

Pop. 7,166. On the Seneca River and the New York State Barge Canal; on the New York Central and Hudson River Railroad. Seneca Falls is in an agricultural and fruit-growing region. The chief industrial establishments are machine shops, woolen factories, fire-engine and pump works, grist mill and furniture factory. Its shipments are chiefly farm products, fruit and dairy products, pumps, and fire-engines.

Stamford, Conn. Vol. 25.

Pop. 56,765, for the town. It is located on Long Island Sound; on the New York, New Haven and Hartford Railroad, 30 miles northeast of New York City. The harbor is large enough for large Sound vessels. The surrounding country is devoted mainly to agriculture, but the city has large manufacturing interests and is the commercial center of an extensive region.

White Plains, N. Y. Vol. 29.

Pop. 35,830. White Plains is the county-seat of Westchester County. It is located on the Harlem Division of the New York Central and Hudson River Railroad, about 20 miles from the central part of New York City. It has several manufactories and has grown rapidly as a residential suburb.

The second aim was to survey the entire school population in a community within the given grades. This condition was satisfied except in Stamford and White Plains. In Stamford about 120 twelfth grade pupils were omitted because of a misunderstanding concerning the amount of materials needed, the correction not being made in time to have these pupils take part. In White Plains the supervision of the work was undertaken by one teacher and not all the classes were included. The principal of the school examined the list of classes which were included and reported that he saw no reason to believe the classes used were not representative of all the English classes for each grade in the school.

The third aim concerned the number of pupils to be surveyed. The original aim was to secure approximately 1,000 pupils per grade. This was attained only in the tenth grade. In the seventh, eighth, and ninth grades between 800 and 900 pupils took part; in the eleventh grade the number was more than 400; and in the twelfth grade, more than 300. Table III gives the total number of returns for each grade by sexes, individually and combined.

TABLE III

TOTAL NUMBER OF RETURNS ON COMPOSITION TITLE PREFERENCES FOR EACH GRADE

Grade	Boys	Girls	Boys and Girls
7	1,199	1,320	2,519
8	1,205	1,335	2,540
9	1,428	1,355	2,783
10	2,311	2,109	4,420
11	625	707	1,332
12	542	410	952
Total	7,310	7,236	14,546

Inasmuch as each pupil made returns from three different lists, these totals, divided by three, give the approximate number of pupils participating, as indicated in Table IV.

TABLE IV
Approximate Number of Pupils Who Used Lists of Titles

Grade	Number	Grade	Number
7	840	10	1,470
8	845	11	440
9	925	12	315

This approximation errs in the direction of being too small. Occasionally pupils were absent from class when one or two of the lists were assigned. This consideration is eliminated by dividing by three to secure an average; for example, if one pupil wrote on lists A and C, but was absent for B, while another pupil missed A and C but wrote on B, the average of the contributions is one pupil, although two have done the work. Such cases were in no sense abundant.

Since fourth year English is generally an elective subject, there are fewer pupils taking it than if it were required. Also, the upper classes are generally smaller than other classes because of two conditions: an increasing population makes the younger classes larger and pupils increasingly tend to drop out of school as they grow older. These conditions account for the smaller number of pupils in the two upper grades of the high school.

In White Plains and Stamford only pupils of the tenth, eleventh, and twelfth grades participated in an endeavor to build up the totals for these grades.

CHAPTER III

INTERESTS INDICATED BY THE TITLES OF FREE CHOICE COMPOSITIONS

In the investigation of the topics pupils prefer to write about, they were asked first to write a composition upon any topic of their own suggestion. No topics or titles were offered by the teacher. When these compositions were handed in, each teacher made a list of the titles and indicated the sex of the authors. For convenience these compositions were called Free Choice Compositions.

Some teachers failed to return these lists. Some lists were discarded because of omissions which made sex identification impossible. The total numbers of returns from boys and girls combined are given in Table V.

TABLE V

TOTAL NUMBER OF PUPILS WRITING FREE CHOICE COMPOSITIONS

Grade	Huntington	Kalamazoo	Seneca Falls	Stamford*	Total	Grand Total
7	170	424	69	...	663	
8	175	607	57	...	839	
9	217	544	93	...	854	
10	90	515	53	536	1,194	
11	143**	59	37	73	312	
12	0	45	41	71	157	4,019

*Stamford did not undertake any of the work with seventh, eighth, or ninth grades.
**83 returns were sent in as grade "XI and XII."

THE CLASSIFICATION OF TITLES OF FREE CHOICE COMPOSITIONS

Classification of these topics on the basis of the definitions used in Table I would have the advantage of making comparisons with the results obtained by the use of the A, B, and C lists. Accordingly, an attempt was made to classify about 150 tenth grade titles according to Table I. The following facts seemed apparent: (1) classifications by means of Table I could be made if additions were made to a few of the definitions; and (2) a few classifications should be added to the list. Elaborations of twelve of the definitions in Table I were made as follows:

2. Add to the definition, "The word 'adventure' appears in the title or is suggested by such words or phrases as exciting, a race, or a haunted house."
7. Add, "To include topics about patriotism or qualities allied to it."
10. Add, "Topics concerned with character in general or some specific aspect of it."
13. Add, "Any title suggesting how to make ...."
18. This topic was combined with No. 2 (Adventure) since titles often did not indicate the differences which the two definitions specify in Table I. In particular, it was often impossible to determine whether or not an indefinite title was used to relate an adventure.
19. Add, "To include hobbies, picnics, parties, and the like, which are not definite enough to be classified elsewhere."
20. Add, "Or the lives of authors."
23. Add, "To include composers."
24. This title was combined with No. 5 (Athletics) because it was so often impossible to discern whether or not titles included organized games.
26. Add, "Stressing the first person—what he did or experienced."
30. Add, "Or the general topic of education in any of its phases."
35. Add, "To include visits which cannot be classified elsewhere."

Topics unclassifiable by the revised Table I were listed. A review of these lists indicated a relatively large number of titles concerned with the following topics:

Aviation or airplanes.
Farming or experiences on visits to farms.
Seasons of the year.
Vacations—particularly summer vacations.

Accordingly, these four classifications were added to the list with the following respective designations: A, F, S, and V. A fifth classification included all the unclassified titles under the heading, Miscellaneous.

Tables VI, VII, and VIII give rank order lists of the free choice composition titles according to the classifications given above for boys, girls, and boys and girls combined, respectively. The results were tabulated by grades and given in per cents of the total number of titles for each grade. It is obvious that the small number of cases in the eleventh and twelfth grades makes the results in those grades inconclusive. Nevertheless, the lists for these grades do not show any violent tendencies away from the major trends apparent throughout the lower grades.

TABLE VI
RANK ORDER LIST OF BOYS' FREE CHOICE COMPOSITION INTERESTS

A Rank Order List of 2,040 Boys' Interests as Indicated by the Titles of Their Free Choice Compositions. Interests Are Ranked by Grades in the Order of the Per Cent of Pupils' Selections of Each Interest

GRADE 7		GRADE 8		GRADE 9		GRADE 10		GRADE 11		GRADE 12	
Title	%	Title	%	Title	%	Title	%	Title	%	Title	%
Adventure	21.9	Sports	20.5	Sports	22.2	Sports	26.8	Sports	20.9	Adventure	15.6
Sports	19.5	Adventure	12.4	Adventure	13.6	Adventure	12.4	Misc.	12.7	Sports	12.6
Animals	11.0	Travel	8.6	Aviation	11.8	Aviation	9.8	Adventure	11.4	School	11.6
Travel	9.2	Per. Exp.	8.2	Misc.	7.2	Misc.	9.0	School	5.7	Travel	7.8
Farms	4.9	Animals	6.2	Per. Exp.	6.6	Travel	4.5	Aviation	5.7	Aviation	7.8
Misc.	4.5	Leisure	5.2	Travel	5.9	School	4.1	Cur. Events	5.1	Misc.	4.8
Per. Exp.	4.0	Misc.	4.7	Animals	3.8	Machines	3.5	Per. Exp.	5.1	Vocations	3.9
Leisure	3.7	Aviation	4.4	Leisure	3.4	Per. Exp.	3.3	Travel	5.1	Leisure	3.9
Aviation	3.1	History	3.7	Science	2.9	Leisure	3.2	Seasons	4.4	Science	3.9
Vacation	2.4	Science	3.0	Machines	2.5	Animals	2.8	Science	3.8	Cur. Events	2.9
Fam. People	2.1	Vacation	2.2	History	2.3	Science	2.8	Civics	2.5	Machines	2.9
History	2.1	Fam. People	2.0	Handwork	2.0	Vocations	2.3	History	2.5	Music	2.9
Literature	1.8	School	1.7	School	2.0	History	2.0	Leisure	2.5	Per. Exp.	2.9
Science	1.5	Vocations	1.5	Vacation	1.8	Literature	2.0	Literature	2.5	Farms	2.9
Cur. Events	1.2	Cur. Events	1.2	Vocations	1.6	Seasons	2.0	Handwork	1.9	Fam. People	1.9
Vocations	1.0	Literature	1.2	Ethics	1.1	Soc. Prob.	1.5	Machines	1.9	People	1.9
Home Life	1.0	Employment	1.2	Fam. People	.9	Fam. People	.8	Music	1.3	Children	1.0
Machines	1.0	Handwork	1.0	Cur. Events	.9	Music	.8	Vocations	.6	Ethics	1.0
People	1.0	Humor	1.0	Literature	.9	Art	.7	Animals	.6	Health	1.0
Fairy Tales	.6	People	1.0	Industries	.9	Civics	.7	Fam. People	.6	History	1.0
Handwork	.6	Farms	1.0	Employment	.9	Cur. Events	.7	Ethics	.6	Humor	1.0
Seasons	.6	Art	.7	Civics	.7	Ethics	.7	Health	.6	Literature	1.0
Civics	.3	Ethics	.7	Home Life	.7	Handwork	.7	Industries	.6	Industries	1.0
Ethics	.3	Get Rich	.7	Children	.7	Industries	.7	Soc. Prob.	.6	Employment	1.0
Music	.3	Home Life	.7	Music	.4	Vacation	.5	Farms	.6	Vacation	1.0
Employment	.3	Machines	.7	People	.4	Farms	.5			Seasons	1.0
School	.3	Industries	.7	Religion	.4	Proverbs	.3				
		Soc. Prob.	.7	Seasons	.4	Employment	.3				
		Seasons	.7	Health	.2	Children	.2				
		Civics	.5	Humor	.2	Get Rich	.2				
		Music	.5	Proverbs	.2	Health	.2				
		Proverbs	.5	Sentiment	.2	Home Life	.2				
		Fairy Tales	.2	Sympathy	.2	Religion	.2				
		Health	.2								
		Win Prizes	.2								
	100.2		99.6		99.6		100.4		99.8		100.1
	N—328		N—405		N—442		N—604		N—158		N—103

Interests Shown by Titles of Free Choice Compositions

TABLE VII

RANK ORDER LIST OF GIRLS' FREE CHOICE COMPOSITION INTERESTS

A Rank Order List of 1,979 Girls' Interests as Indicated by the Titles of Their Free Choice Compositions. Interests Are Ranked by Grades in the Order of the Per Cent of Pupils' Selections of Each Interest

GRADE 7		GRADE 8		GRADE 9		GRADE 10		GRADE 11		GRADE 12	
Title	%	Title	%	Title	%	Title	%	Title	%	Title	%
Adventure	20.0	Adventure	14.8	Adventure	13.4	Travel	14.8	Adventure	13.0	Vocations	11.1
Travel	14.6	Travel	14.0	Sports	12.9	Adventure	13.2	School	10.4	Travel	11.1
Sports	9.8	Sports	11.0	Travel	12.1	Sports	11.0	Misc.	10.4	Adventure	9.3
Leisure	9.0	Leisure	9.0	School	8.2	Leisure	8.5	Sports	9.8	Misc.	9.3
Vacation	8.7	Animals	8.1	Misc.	8.0	Misc.	7.3	Travel	9.1	Sports	7.4
Animals	7.5	Per. Exp.	5.5	Leisure	6.6	School	6.1	Seasons	5.8	Ethics	5.6
Per. Exp.	4.5	Literature	5.1	Per. Exp.	5.8	Per. Exp.	5.1	Literature	5.2	Music	5.6
Misc.	3.9	Vacation	4.2	Literature	4.4	Seasons	4.8	Leisure	4.5	School	5.6
School	3.6	Misc.	3.7	Seasons	3.2	Literature	2.9	Music	3.9	Science	5.6
Home Life	3.3	Vocations	3.0	Vocations	2.2	History	2.7	History	3.2	Soc. Prob.	5.6
History	2.4	History	3.0	Animals	2.2	Vocations	2.5	Vocations	2.6	History	3.7
Science	2.1	School	2.5	Music	2.2	Animals	2.5	Per. Exp.	2.6	Leisure	3.7
Fam. People	1.5	Science	2.1	Vacation	1.9	Science	2.5	Soc. Prob.	2.6	Literature	3.7
Children	1.2	Fam. People	1.2	Aviation	1.9	Vacation	2.4	Vacation	2.6	Per. Exp.	3.7
Humor	1.2	Ethics	1.2	Fam. People	1.5	Music	1.7	Animals	2.0	Seasons	3.7
Literature	1.2	Get Rich	1.2	Ethics	1.5	Aviation	1.7	Science	2.0	Cur. Events	1.8
Soc. Prob.	.9	Soc. Prob.	1.2	Home Life	1.5	Civics	1.2	Civics	1.3	Health	1.8
Cur. Events	.6	Seasons	1.2	History	1.2	Ethics	1.2	Fam. People	1.3	Industries	1.8
Handwork	.6	Farms	1.2	Science	1.2	Humor	1.2	Cur. Events	1.3		
Industries	.6	Home Life	.9	Children	.7	Machines	.8	Ethics	1.3		
People	.6	Children	.7	Civics	.7	Art	.7	Handwork	1.3		
Farms	.6	Humor	.7	Health	.7	Get Rich	.7	Machines	1.3		
Vocations	.3	Music	.7	People	.7	Farms	.7	Aviation	1.3		
Ethics	.3	Employment	.7	Employment	.7	Children	.5	Art	.6		
Health	.3	Win Prizes	.7	Farms	.7	Fam. People	.5	People	.6		
Machines	.3	Cur. Events	.5	Cur. Events	.5	Home Life	.5				
Seasons	.3	Proverbs	.5	Fairy Tales	.5	People	.5				
		Art	.2	Handwork	.5	Employment	.5				
		Civics	.2	Religion	.5	Cur. Events	.3				
		Music	.2	Soc. Prob.	.5	Handwork	.3				
		Handwork	.2	Art	.2	Religion	.3				
		Health	.2	Get Rich	.2	Health	.2				
		Industries	.2	Humor	.2	Industries	.2				
		Religion	.2	Industries	.2	Soc. Prob.	.2				
		Aviation	.2	Proverbs	.2	Sympathy	.2				
				Sympathy	.2						
	99.8		100.2		99.8		100.4		100.0		100.1
	N—335		N—434		N—412		N—590		N—154		N—54

TABLE VIII

Rank Order List of Boys' and Girls' Free Choice Composition Interests

Rank Order List of 4,029 Boys' and Girls' Interests as Indicated by the Titles of Their Free Choice Compositions. Interests Are Ranked by Grades in the Order of the Per Cent of Pupils' Selections of Each Interest

Grade 7		Grade 8		Grade 9		Grade 10		Grade 11		Grade 12	
Title	%	Title	%	Title	%	Title	%	Title	%	Title	%
Adventure	21.1	Sports	15.6	Sports	17.7	Sports	19.0	Sports	15.4	Adventure	13.4
Sports	14.6	Adventure	13.6	Adventure	13.5	Adventure	12.8	Adventure	12.2	Sports	10.1
Travel	11.9	Travel	11.4	Travel	8.9	Travel	9.6	Misc.	11.5	School	9.6
Animals	9.2	Animals	7.2	Misc.	7.6	Misc.	8.1	School	8.0	Travel	8.9
Leisure	6.3	Leisure	7.2	Aviation	7.0	Leisure	5.8	Travel	7.0	Vocations	6.4
Vacation	5.6	Per. Exp.	6.8	Per. Exp.	6.2	Aviation	5.8	Seasons	5.1	Misc.	6.4
Per. Exp.	4.2	Misc.	4.2	School	5.0	School	5.1	Literature	3.8	Aviation	5.1
Misc.	4.2	History	3.3	Leisure	4.9	Per. Exp.	4.2	Per. Exp.	3.8	Science	4.5
Farms	2.7	Literature	3.2	Animals	3.0	Seasons	3.4	Aviation	3.5	Leisure	3.8
History	2.3	Vacation	3.2	Literature	2.6	Animals	2.7	Aviation	3.5	Music	3.8
Home Life	2.1	Science	2.5	Science	2.1	Science	2.7	Cur. Events	3.2	Per. Exp.	3.2
School	2.0	Vocations	2.3	Vocations	1.9	Vocations	2.4	History	2.9	Cur. Events	2.6
Fam. People	1.8	Aviation	2.3	Vacation	1.9	Literature	2.4	Science	2.9	Ethics	2.6
Science	1.8	School	2.1	History	1.8	History	2.3	Music	2.6	History	1.9
Literature	1.5	Fam. People	1.6	Seasons	1.8	Machines	2.2	Civics	1.9	Literature	1.9
Aviation	1.5	Farms	1.1	Ethics	1.3	Vacation	1.0	Vocations	1.6	Machines	1.9
Cur. Events	.9	Ethics	1.0	Handwork	1.3	Music	1.0	Handwork	1.6	Soc. Prob.	1.9
People	.8	Get Rich	1.0	Machines	1.3	Civics	.9	Machines	1.6	Seasons	1.9
Vocations	.6	Employment	1.0	Music	1.3	Ethics	.9	Soc. Prob.	1.6	Farms	1.9
Children	.6	Soc. Prob.	1.0	Fam. People	1.2	Soc. Prob.	.8	Animals	1.3	Fam. People	1.3
Handwork	.6	Seasons	1.0	Home Life	1.0	Art	.7	Vacation	1.3	Health	1.3
Humor	.6	Cur. Events	.8	Employment	.8	Fam. People	.7	Fam. People	1.0	Industries	1.3
Machines	.6	Home Life	.8	Civics	.7	Humor	.6	Ethics	1.0	People	1.3
Soc. Prob.	.4	Humor	.8	Cur. Events	.7	Farms	.6	Art	.3	Children	.6
Seasons	.4	Handwork	.6	Children	.6	Cur. Events	.5	Health	.3	Humor	.6
Ethics	.3	Music	.6	Industries	.6	Handwork	.5	Industries	.3	Employment	.6
Fairy Tales	.3	Art	.5	People	.5	Get Rich	.4	People	.3	Vacation	.6
Industries	.3	Industries	.5	Health	.5	Employment	.4	Farms	.3		
Civics	.1	People	.5	Religion	.5	Industries	.1				
Health	.1	Proverbs	.5	Farms	.4	Children	.3				
Music	.1	Win Prizes	.5	Fairy Tales	.2	Home Life	.3				
Employment	.1	Children	.4	Humor	.2	People	.2				
		Civics	.4	Proverbs	.2	Religion	.2				
		Machines	.4	Soc. Prob.	.2	Health	.2				
		Fairy Tales	.2	Sympathy	.2	Proverbs	.2				
		Health	.2	Art	.1	Sympathy	.1				
		Religion	.1	Get Rich	.1						
				Sentiment	.1						
	100.0		100.4		100.0		99.5		99.8		99.4
	N—663		N—839		N—854		N—1194		N—312		N—157

Analysis of the Rank Order Lists

Boys

Sports and Adventure are ranked highest in all grades except the eleventh, where the group of Miscellaneous Topics slightly outranks Adventure. Travel ranks high in all grades. Sports, Adventure, and Travel account for more than 40 per cent of all choices through the tenth grade and for more than 35 per cent in the eleventh and twelfth grades. Animals provides a much larger number of titles in the lower than in the upper grades. Aviation and Personal Experience stand high, especially in the eighth, ninth, and tenth grades. School, as a topic for written compositions, provides a larger percentage of the titles in the last three grades than in the first three.

Girls

Adventure, Travel, and Sports are the three highest ranking topics through the tenth grade. They rank among the first five in all grades, accounting for from 45 per cent of all choices in the seventh to 28 per cent in the twelfth. Leisure and Personal Experience are near the top of the list from the seventh grade through the tenth.

Boys and Girls Combined

Sports and Adventure, accounting for 25 to 35 per cent of all choices, hold the highest two positions in all grades. Travel ranks third through the tenth grade, and among the first five in both the eleventh grade and the twelfth grade. Miscellaneous Titles tends to move toward the top of the lists in the upper grades. This seems to be due to an increasingly wider range of interests that are not classifiable in sufficient amounts to warrant adding new categories to the list. School is used more as pupils progress through school.

Moving from the seventh to the twelfth grade, from 47 to 32 per cent of the pupils of their own choice prefer to write about Sports, Adventure, or Travel. The other 50 per cent of the choices are very much divided. Animals and Vacation are much less frequently used in the upper than in the lower grades.

Random Lists of Titles

Random lists of titles for the seventh grade through the ninth were made by listing every twentieth title on all the lists turned in. Certain qualities stand out. These titles show many shades of interest which are hidden by the broad definitions of our categories.

A reading of the lists gives an impression of a large variety of interests with many titles worded to capture the interest of the reader.

Appendix IV contains the grade lists of titles which were not classified.

RANDOM LISTS OF TITLES OF FREE CHOICE COMPOSITIONS

Seventh Grade Pupils

A Child Visits a Doctor
Going on a Fishing Trip*
Why I Like Stamps*
A Movie That I Liked
A Fishing Trip
Passing into Junior High School
My Visit to a Paper Mill
The Skating Party
Birds
Sweet Tooth*
A Walk That Will Not Be Forgotten*
An Unusual Ghost*
A Trip to Japan
The Wind
Education
Westward Bound
Astronomy
How I Fell Through the Ice*
My Dog
My Mistake in the Store*
My Trip to Niagara Falls
My Pet Dog*
Friendly Siskins
Dogs and How to Take Care of Them*
Going to School*
A Rainy Day*
Making Taffy
A Funny Story
The Graf Zeppelin*
The Prize
My Visit on a Battleship*
On Grandpa's Farm*
Sledding*
Halloween Night
When Pranks Are Played*

*Boy

Eighth Grade Pupils

Boat Racing on the Mississippi*
A Basketball Game*
Travel
My School
Lady Grey's Slippers
Trips I Would Like to Take
A Girl Scout Rally Night
The Next World War*
How Dumb Animals Should Be Treated
An Old Soldier*
My Rock Garden
The First Lesson I Took in Swimming
A Ghost in a Deserted House
A Wonderful Thing
A Book for Girls
Why I Should Like to Travel
How Boat-Making Grew
Living on a Farm*
How to Play a Game
What I Do in Summer*
A Trip I Would Like to Take*
The Great North*
At the Circus
My Favorite Author
Shenandoah Caverns
My Trip to Massachusetts and to Maine*
Spooks*
A Day of Mishaps
Sports—Both Winter and Summer*
Girl Scouts
Brush
A Sure Sign of Spring
My Pet
Why Johnny Likes Spring*
Going Hiking
The Fire
There's No Place Like Home*
A Trip to The Mountains
The Lost Dog
How I Spend My Vacation
My Uncle's Farm
Never Again*
A Fishing Trip*
Safety First*

*Boy

Our Cat*
The Flying Squirrel
My Halloween Experience*
How I Learned to Swim
A Day of Mishaps

Ninth Grade Pupils

The Slaves of Old Rome
A Trip to Fremont*
How I Got My Dog*
A Trip to Old Baldy
My First Trip to Grand Rapids
How Our Fun Was Spoiled*
An Automobile Trip*
The Gold Medal Dog
Christmas Joy
A Book Review
Why I Like Spring
Our Football Team
A Trip I Would Like to Take
Ants
The Lady and The Tiger
An Old Horn*
The Fire at the Ball Park*
The Advantages of a Commercial Course
The Dogs of the North*
Elias Howe's Invention
Using a Typewriter
Teaching
Georges Clemenceau*
Aviation
Imagination
The Old Farm Horse
The Squirrel*
Mayor Walker and His Associates*
My Trip to Cincinnati
My Memories
Nature*
Fair Play*
Ludwig Beethoven
Skiing
Boat Races in Detroit*
Traffic in the Halls
Hurrying to School on a Holiday*
My Visit to the Art Gallery

*Boy

A Sleigh Ride Party
Ted's Experience in the Woods*
The Kodak Club*
My Life on the Farm
Sports
A Day Spent in Pleasure*
Schooling*
Reading in General
The Talkies

CONCLUSIONS CONCERNING THE TOPICS WHICH PUPILS THEMSELVES SUGGEST FOR WRITTEN COMPOSITIONS

1. These data indicate that the sexes show a high degree of uniformity in their major interest. The half or more of the boys and the girls who did not write upon the major interests show differences between the sexes in the variety of their minor interests.

2. The chief interests of boys and girls, combined or taken separately, when they are free to select their own topics, are: Adventure, Sports, and Travel.

3. The younger pupils of secondary school age also use Animals and Vacation as topics of major interest.

4. Older pupils of secondary school age find School increasingly interesting as a topic for written compositions.

5. Pupils of secondary schools appear to have a variety of interests suitable for use as composition topics of their own choosing. In no case did less than 50 per cent of the pupils choose topics other than the three most commonly chosen.

6. The increase in the per cent of unclassified topics in the upper grades indicates an increasing range of interests as pupils progress through secondary schools.

7. Even the youngest secondary school pupils appear to have a background of interests which can be relied upon for topics for compositions.

* Boy

CHAPTER IV

WRITTEN COMPOSITION INTERESTS INDICATED BY PUPILS' CHOICES FROM LISTS OF TITLES

This investigation of the topics about which pupils prefer to write compositions utilized the A, B, and C lists of titles described in Chapter II. The method of selecting the titles to represent thirty-six different categories of interests and the order in which the titles were placed on the lists are fully described in Chapter II. Samples of the lists are given in Appendix II.

These lists were used in composition classes for the three written assignments immediately following the Free Choice Composition assignment. Teachers were asked to distribute the A list for the first written assignment after the Free Choice Composition was done, and to ask the pupils to write their compositions, using any title on the list. Pupils retained the lists until the compositions were "handed in." With the compositions, pupils returned the stub at the bottom of the list. On this stub the pupil gave seven items of information: age, sex, and grade in school; and the numbers of (a) the title he chose for his composition, (b) the title he liked next best, (c) the title he liked least or disliked most, and (d) the title he disliked next most. Only the stubs were collected for this inquiry; the teacher retained the compositions. Names were not asked for; it was thought that a pupil would feel more free to make a frank choice if his identity were hidden than if he were to feel that those who tabulated his response would connect his name with his choice. The B and C lists were used similarly for the next two assignments.

Table IX gives the numbers of pupils in each city who used each list. The data are given by grades for boys separately, for girls separately, and for boys and girls combined. Since each pupil was asked to write three compositions, an equivalent of approximately 4,845 pupils took part in this investigation. This number is too small an approximation, however, since some pupils, on account of absence, turned in only one or two compositions.

TABLE IX
Returns on Composition Title Preferences*

Grade	City	Boys Form A	B	C	Total	Girls Form A	B	C	Total	Boys and Girls Form A	B	C	Total
7	K	284	282	284	850	311	317	308	936	595	599	592	1,786
	SF	39	39	39	117	32	32	32	96	71	71	71	213
	H	78	79	75	232	95	99	94	288	173	178	169	520
	Total	401	400	398	1,199	438	448	434	1,320	839	848	832	2,519
8	K	288	298	282	868	320	325	327	972	608	623	609	1,840
	SF	29	31	28	88	23	21	23	67	52	52	51	155
	H	77	88	84	249	101	98	97	296	178	186	181	545
	Total	394	417	394	1,205	444	444	447	1,335	838	861	841	2,540
9	K	314	308	299	921	334	326	336	996	648	634	635	1,917
	SF	57	57	56	170	36	12	36	84	93	69	92	254
	H	115	112	110	337	93	92	90	275	208	204	200	612
	Total	486	477	465	1,428	463	430	462	1,355	949	907	927	2,783
10	K	239	248	251	738	275	270	259	804	514	518	510	1,542
	SF	34	30	30	94	26	24	24	74	60	54	54	168
	H	49	51	58	158	57	71	68	196	106	122	126	354
	WP	54	66	72	192	31	39	41	111	85	105	113	303
	S	303	416	410	1,129	258	347	319	924	561	763	729	2,053
	Total	679	811	821	2,311	647	751	711	2,109	1,326	1,562	1,532	4,420
11	K	34	34	34	102	48	47	46	141	82	81	80	243
	SF	14	14	14	42	23	23	22	68	37	37	36	110
	H	38	32	47	117	41	35	41	117	79	67	88	234
	WP	45	52	47	144	33	59	53	145	78	111	100	289
	S	66	80	74	220	74	77	85	236	140	157	159	456
	Total	197	212	216	625	219	241	247	707	416	453	463	1,332
12	K	32	30	31	93	19	18	17	54	51	48	48	147
	SF	23	20	19	62	23	24	24	71	46	44	43	133
	H	25	25	25	75	34	34	34	102	59	59	59	177
	WP	35	30	35	100	33	36	32	101	68	66	67	201
	S	71	72	69	212	25	29	28	82	96	101	97	294
	Total	186	177	179	542	134	141	135	410	320	318	314	952
Grand totals		2,433	2,494	2,473	7,310	2,345	2,455	2,436	7,236	4,688	4,949	4,909	14,546

* Designations for cities are as follows: K—Kalamazoo. SF—Seneca Falls. H—Huntington. WP—White Plains. S—Stamford.

Treatment of the Data

A median rating for each title category was computed by assigning B a value of 5; NB, 4; no choice, 3; NL, 2; L, 1. These values were considered the mid-points of the intervals for which they stand, for example, 3 means 2.5 to 3.5; and it was assumed that the ratings in each interval were evenly distributed. From the resulting medians, the rank order lists of reported interests found in Tables X to XXVII, inclusive, were compiled.

A median of 3.000 indicates a neutral position between liking and disliking, since that median is the value assigned to a category whenever a pupil has not rated it. Since pupils were asked to rate only four items of a list of thirty-six, the medians cluster around 3.000.[1]

In order to interpret the data correctly, it should be borne in mind, when these tables are read, that "like" and "dislike" refer to the one fact that pupils like or dislike to write about these topics; in other words, pupils like or dislike to use the titles representative of the various categories of interests for titles of written compositions. When the phrase "interested in" appears hereafter in the interpretations of the data of these studies, it will refer to writing about some topic for compositions, and to nothing else. The importance of this distinction can be seen readily in the category of interest which is most commonly disliked in all grades for both boys and girls, as shown in Tables X to XXVII. This category is Sentiment. By definition it is "love for or interest in someone of the opposite sex." The proper interpretation is that there is no topic in our list of thirty-six which the vast number of boys and girls are less interested in writing about. The aversion to it as a topic for written composition is such that out of the thirty-six topics there is no other for which so many of them have selected to signify a definite dislike.

In addition to the medians, these tables give the per cents (correct to the nearest one-tenth of one per cent) of pupils rating a category as B, NB, no choice, NL, and L. Three lists of interests are given for each grade, one for boys and girls together, one for boys, and one for girls.

[1] By definition it would be theoretically possible for a title to have a value of 3.000 when no preference is shown for it. However, where such a median appears in these lists, it is not due to this condition but to the fact that the preferences for or against a title were so evenly divided that they neutralized each other.

TABLE X
Rank Order List of Composition Title Ratings by 2,519 Seventh Grade Boys and Girls

Rank	Title No.	Title	Median	Per Cent of Choices per Weight				
				5	4	3	2	1
1	35	Travel................	3.080	9.8	5.4	82.8	.8	1.2
2	2	Adventure............	3.065	8.7	5.0	83.6	1.5	1.3
3	24	Outdoor Activities......	3.054	6.3	4.6	87.6	1.0	.6
4	3	Animals..............	3.053	6.1	5.5	86.0	1.5	1.0
5	12	Getting Rich..........	3.046	7.4	4.8	83.0	1.9	2.9
6	19	Leisure Activities......	3.036	4.7	4.6	87.6	1.2	1.9
7	20	Literature............	3.035	3.5	4.8	89.7	1.0	1.0
8.5	9	Current Events........	3.028	4.5	6.1	83.5	2.9	3.1
8.5	10	Ethics................	3.028	3.2	3.3	92.1	.8	.6
10	8	Famous People........	3.021	3.4	4.7	87.5	2.0	2.4
11	26	Personal Experience....	3.015	3.6	3.1	89.3	2.4	1.7
12	28	Pupil Employment.....	3.014	3.1	2.5	91.5	1.3	1.8
13	5	Athletics..............	3.011	1.6	2.5	93.7	1.2	1.0
14	17	Humorous Anecdotes...	3.010	1.8	3.1	91.8	1.9	1.3
15	34	Sympathy.............	3.009	1.3	1.9	95.1	.9	.8
16	29	Religion..............	3.006	2.2	1.8	93.2	1.3	1.6
17	16	Home Life............	3.005	2.6	2.8	90.1	2.2	2.3
18	36	Winning Prizes........	2.998	.8	2.5	93.0	2.3	1.4
19	1	Vocations.............	2.996	1.6	1.5	93.0	1.9	2.0
20	30	School................	2.993	2.1	2.4	89.7	2.6	3.2
21	4	Art...................	2.989	1.0	.9	94.0	2.3	1.7
22	22	Modern Industries......	2.987	1.7	1.2	91.9	3.0	2.3
23.5	11	Fairy Tales...........	2.982	1.6	2.0	89.5	3.6	3.3
23.5	15	Historical Events......	2.982	2.5	1.8	88.1	3.2	4.4
25	13	Handwork............	2.977	1.4	1.5	90.0	3.5	3.7
26	7	Civics................	2.973	.2	.6	93.3	3.5	2.4
27.5	18	Indefinite Titles........	2.970	2.7	3.5	82.6	6.1	5.1
27.5	27	Proverbs.............	2.970	1.0	1.7	89.2	4.6	3.6
29	23	Music................	2.969	1.8	2.3	86.4	5.1	4.4
30.5	31	Science...............	2.968	.6	1.9	89.2	4.7	3.7
30.5	33	Social Problems........	2.968	.6	1.4	90.1	4.0	3.9
32	21	Machines.............	2.967	1.0	1.3	89.4	4.4	4.0
33	25	People................	2.965	.8	1.2	90.0	3.8	4.4
34	6	Children..............	2.963	1.9	2.4	85.0	5.0	5.7
35	14	Health................	2.954	.8	.4	89.4	4.7	4.8
36	32	Sentiment.............	2.935	1.1	2.3	82.4	5.7	8.5

Legend: B—5; NB—4; No Choice—3; NL—2; L—1.

TABLE XI
Rank Order List of Composition Title Ratings by 2,540 Eighth Grade Boys and Girls

Rank	Title No.	Title	Median	Per Cent of Choices per Weight				
				5	4	3	2	1
1	35	Travel...............	3.102	11.3	7.0	79.6	1.2	.9
2	2	Adventure...........	3.069	9.5	4.8	83.0	1.6	1.1
3	24	Outdoor Activities......	3.053	6.0	5.0	87.3	.9	.8
4	9	Current Events........	3.046	5.9	5.5	84.5	2.3	1.7
5	10	Ethics...............	3.041	4.4	4.6	89.4	.6	1.0
6	3	Animals..............	3.040	4.8	5.2	87.1	1.7	1.3
7.5	12	Getting Rich..........	3.030	5.1	5.1	84.6	2.6	2.6
7.5	19	Leisure Activities......	3.030	4.0	4.8	88.0	1.8	1.6
9	20	Literature............	3.029	2.9	4.3	90.8	1.1	.9
10	5	Athletics.............	3.023	2.9	3.5	91.4	1.2	1.0
11	26	Personal Experience....	3.018	3.1	3.6	89.7	2.3	1.2
12	8	Famous People........	3.016	4.0	3.9	87.1	2.3	2.7
13	28	Pupil Employment.....	3.012	2.3	2.4	92.7	1.2	1.3
14	34	Sympathy............	3.009	1.7	2.1	94.1	1.3	.9
15	29	Religion.............	3.005	2.1	1.8	93.1	1.4	1.7
16	1	Vocations............	3.004	2.5	2.6	90.5	2.3	2.0
17	16	Home Life...........	3.002	2.8	1.8	91.2	2.4	1.7
18	17	Humorous Anecdotes...	3.001	1.4	2.8	91.9	2.4	1.6
19	36	Winning Prizes........	2.994	.8	2.2	93.0	2.2	1.8
20	22	Modern Industries.....	2.992	1.6	1.6	92.3	2.6	2.0
21	15	Historical Events......	2.990	2.5	2.2	88.9	3.6	2.8
22	30	School...............	2.987	2.2	2.0	89.2	2.8	3.7
23	4	Art..................	2.983	.7	.7	94.0	2.5	2.2
24	7	Civics...............	2.978	.5	.9	93.0	2.8	2.8
25	13	Handwork............	2.974	1.0	1.6	90.0	3.5	3.8
26	23	Music................	2.971	1.5	3.2	85.6	4.3	5.4
27	31	Science..............	2.970	1.3	1.1	89.9	3.9	3.8
28.5	18	Indefinite Titles.......	2.968	2.0	2.5	85.3	5.6	4.6
28.5	25	People...............	2.968	.8	1.0	90.6	3.9	3.6
30.5	11	Fairy Tales...........	2.967	1.6	1.4	88.3	4.5	4.2
30.5	21	Machines.............	2.967	1.4	1.6	88.2	4.1	4.8
32	27	Proverbs.............	2.965	.9	1.5	89.0	5.1	3.6
33	14	Health...............	2.958	.9	1.0	88.8	4.1	5.3
34	33	Social Problems.......	2.956	.9	.9	88.8	4.4	5.2
35	6	Children.............	2.952	1.4	1.6	86.0	5.2	5.9
36	32	Sentiment............	2.942	1.0	2.2	84.0	4.4	8.5

Legend: B—5; NB—4; No Choice—3; NL—2; L—1.

TABLE XII

Rank Order List of Composition Title Ratings by 2,783 Ninth Grade Boys and Girls

Rank	Title No.	Title	Median	Per Cent of Choices per Weight				
				5	4	3	2	1
1	35	Travel..............	3.086	8.9	6.9	82.6	.9	.7
2	2	Adventure............	3.059	7.6	4.7	85.4	1.4	.9
3	24	Outdoor Activities.....	3.053	6.1	4.6	88.1	.9	.4
4	10	Ethics................	3.039	3.8	4.5	90.4	.8	.5
5	19	Leisure Activities......	3.033	4.1	4.2	89.0	1.2	1.4
6	5	Athletics.............	3.029	3.6	3.3	91.5	.9	.8
7.5	3	Animals..............	3.028	4.1	4.1	88.5	1.5	1.8
7.5	8	Famous People........	3.028	4.4	4.3	87.2	2.0	1.9
9	20	Literature............	3.024	3.1	3.4	91.3	1.1	1.0
10	26	Personal Experience....	3.023	3.8	4.0	88.3	1.6	2.1
11	9	Current Events........	3.018	3.6	4.8	86.6	2.7	2.4
12	12	Getting Rich..........	3.015	3.4	4.3	87.2	2.3	2.7
13	28	Pupil Employment.....	3.014	2.7	2.2	92.9	1.6	.7
14	34	Sympathy.............	3.011	1.4	2.0	95.2	.9	.5
15	17	Humorous Anecdotes...	3.010	2.0	3.8	90.2	2.2	1.9
16	16	Home Life............	3.006	2.6	2.2	91.7	2.1	1.4
17	30	School................	2.999	3.2	2.3	89.0	2.6	3.0
18	36	Winning Prizes........	2.996	.8	1.9	93.3	1.8	1.5
19	29	Religion..............	2.995	1.7	1.4	92.9	2.0	2.0
20.5	1	Vocations............	2.994	2.4	2.0	90.1	2.9	2.5
20.5	15	Historic Events........	2.994	3.5	2.7	86.6	3.5	3.7
22.5	18	Indefinite Titles.......	2.988	2.6	2.9	86.5	4.6	3.4
22.5	22	Modern Industries.....	2.988	2.0	1.6	90.5	3.1	2.9
24	4	Art...................	2.984	.7	1.1	93.3	2.5	2.3
25	27	Proverbs.............	2.983	1.1	2.0	90.6	3.6	2.7
26	21	Machines.............	2.980	2.0	2.4	87.6	4.0	4.0
27	14	Health...............	2.979	1.9	3.3	86.0	3.8	5.1
28	25	People...............	2.976	.8	1.1	91.5	3.4	3.1
29	7	Civics................	2.972	1.0	1.1	90.7	2.9	4.2
30	33	Social Problems........	2.971	1.3	1.2	89.6	3.8	3.9
31	23	Music................	2.969	1.7	2.6	86.0	4.5	5.1
32.5	13	Handwork............	2.964	2.0	1.7	86.4	4.6	5.3
32.5	31	Science...............	2.964	1.3	1.0	88.8	4.7	4.1
34	11	Fairy Tales...........	2.962	1.7	1.7	86.6	5.1	5.0
35	6	Children..............	2.946	.8	1.3	86.3	5.3	6.3
36	32	Sentiment............	2.941	.8	1.9	84.5	5.1	7.6

Legend: B—5; NB—4; No Choice—3; NL—2; L—1.

TABLE XIII
Rank Order List of Composition Title Ratings by 4,420 Tenth Grade Boys and Girls

Rank	Title No.	Title	Median	Per Cent of Choices per Weight				
				5	4	3	2	1
1	35	Travel	3.072	8.3	6.2	83.7	.9	.9
2	2	Adventure	3.049	6.0	3.8	88.7	.7	.8
3	24	Outdoor Activities	3.046	5.2	4.5	88.6	1.0	.6
4	5	Athletics	3.042	4.5	4.4	89.8	.9	.5
5.5	10	Ethics	3.037	3.6	3.9	91.7	.5	.2
5.5	19	Leisure Activities	3.037	3.6	3.6	89.7	1.6	1.5
7	20	Literature	3.026	3.3	3.5	91.1	1.0	1.1
8	26	Personal Experience	3.021	3.6	3.3	90.0	1.7	1.4
9	17	Humorous Anecdotes	3.015	1.9	4.1	90.6	1.8	1.5
10	30	School	3.013	3.8	2.2	90.2	2.0	1.7
11.5	1	Vocations	3.012	3.8	2.8	88.9	2.3	2.3
11.5	18	Indefinite Titles	3.012	3.4	3.6	88.1	2.6	2.3
13	3	Animals	3.011	2.2	3.6	90.7	1.9	1.7
14	34	Sympathy	3.010	1.5	2.3	94.3	1.0	.9
15	28	Pupil Employment	3.009	1.8	1.8	94.5	1.1	.7
16.5	12	Getting Rich	3.006	2.9	3.4	88.5	2.5	2.6
16.5	8	Famous People	3.006	2.8	3.4	88.5	2.6	2.7
18	16	Home Life	3.005	2.5	2.0	92.0	2.2	1.4
19	9	Current Events	3.002	2.1	3.4	89.5	2.5	2.5
20	25	People	2.998	1.2	1.3	92.9	2.6	2.1
21	36	Winning Prizes	2.994	1.0	1.6	93.8	2.4	1.2
22	4	Art	2.991	.8	1.5	93.8	2.0	1.9
23	27	Proverbs	2.990	1.1	2.1	91.8	2.9	2.2
24	29	Religion	2.987	.8	.9	94.1	1.6	2.6
25	22	Modern Industries	2.986	1.9	.9	91.9	2.9	2.5
26	23	Music	2.985	2.5	2.9	86.5	4.4	3.7
27	33	Social Problems	2.982	1.2	1.0	92.3	2.6	2.8
28	15	Historic Events	2.974	2.2	2.3	86.5	4.2	4.8
29	31	Science	2.972	1.5	1.4	89.0	3.3	4.6
30	21	Machines	2.970	2.6	2.1	85.2	6.1	4.0
31	7	Civics	2.968	.9	.9	90.9	3.6	3.7
32	13	Handwork	2.960	1.7	1.4	87.0	4.5	5.4
33	14	Health	2.958	1.3	.9	88.3	4.8	4.7
34	11	Fairy Tales	2.957	1.1	1.4	87.3	5.3	5.0
35	6	Children	2.952	1.0	1.0	87.8	4.9	5.3
36	32	Sentiment	2.940	.7	1.4	85.5	4.8	7.6

Legend: B—5; NB—4; No Choice—3; NL—2; L—1.

TABLE XIV
Rank Order List of Composition Title Ratings by 1,332 Eleventh Grade Boys and Girls

Rank	Title No.	Title	Median	Per Cent of Choices per Weight				
				5	4	3	2	1
1	35	Travel................	3.096	10.0	7.4	80.7	1.1	.8
2	5	Athletics..............	3.064	6.1	6.9	85.0	1.4	.7
3	24	Outdoor Activities......	3.048	5.1	5.3	87.6	.9	1.1
4	2	Adventure............	3.038	5.1	4.1	88.5	1.1	1.3
5	10	Ethics................	3.031	3.5	3.6	91.5	.6	.8
6	26	Personal Experience....	3.028	3.8	4.1	89.1	1.6	1.4
7	20	Literature............	3.027	3.5	3.1	91.8	.9	.8
8	30	School................	3.026	4.3	3.1	89.8	1.6	1.2
9	16	Home Life............	3.019	4.1	2.7	89.8	2.1	1.3
10	19	Leisure Activities......	3.018	3.8	3.2	89.5	1.7	2.0
11	17	Humorous Anecdotes...	3.017	2.3	4.1	90.0	2.1	1.5
12	18	Indefinite Titles.......	3.016	3.5	3.9	88.2	2.8	1.7
13.5	3	Animals..............	3.014	3.1	2.9	91.1	1.7	1.4
13.5	34	Sympathy.............	3.014	1.7	2.1	95.0	.7	.5
15.5	1	Vocations.............	3.008	3.6	3.0	88.2	2.4	2.8
15.5	12	Getting Rich..........	3.008	3.3	3.8	87.3	2.8	2.9
17	28	Pupil Employment.....	3.007	1.3	2.2	94.5	1.0	1.1
18	9	Current Events........	3.004	1.3	4.0	90.2	2.5	2.1
19	8	Famous People........	3.002	3.2	3.2	87.6	2.3	3.8
20	21	Machines.............	2.997	4.9	2.6	84.6	4.0	4.0
21	15	Historic Events........	2.995	3.5	2.6	87.0	3.3	3.6
22	23	Music................	2.994	2.0	2.9	89.2	3.5	2.5
23	25	People................	2.992	1.7	2.0	91.5	2.8	2.2
24.5	4	Art...................	2.991	1.2	1.9	92.1	2.6	2.3
24.5	36	Winning Prizes........	2.991	.6	1.6	94.0	1.8	2.1
26	22	Modern Industries.....	2.985	1.8	2.3	89.0	2.9	3.8
27	27	Proverbs..............	2.983	1.6	1.4	91.2	3.2	2.7
28	29	Religion..............	2.974	1.0	.4	92.6	2.8	3.3
29.5	11	Fairy Tales...........	2.967	2.6	2.3	84.7	4.1	6.4
29.5	31	Science...............	2.967	1.7	.9	89.0	4.6	3.8
31	33	Social Problems........	2.966	1.5	.8	89.4	3.8	4.6
32	7	Civics................	2.958	.8	1.4	88.2	5.1	4.5
33	14	Health................	2.945	1.3	1.1	85.9	5.8	6.0
34.5	6	Children..............	2.942	.5	1.4	86.3	5.6	6.2
34.5	13	Handwork............	2.942	1.4	1.2	84.8	6.4	6.2
36	32	Sentiment.............	2.927	.5	1.3	84.2	6.8	7.2

Legend: B—5; NB—4; No Choice—3; NL—2; L—1.

TABLE XV
Rank Order List of Composition Title Ratings by 952 Twelfth Grade Boys and Girls

| Rank | Title No. | Title | Median | Per Cent of Choices per Weight |||||
				5	4	3	2	1
1	35	Travel..............	3.098	8.6	8.5	81.8	.5	.5
2	5	Athletics............	3.063	6.9	5.2	86.5	.9	.4
3	24	Outdoor Activities.....	3.043	4.8	4.3	89.5	.8	.5
4	26	Personal Experience....	3.040	3.9	5.4	88.7	1.2	.9
5	2	Adventure...........	3.035	4.8	3.9	88.8	.9	1.6
6	10	Ethics..............	3.031	3.4	3.9	91.2	.5	1.1
7	17	Humorous Anecdotes...	3.023	2.8	3.8	91.0	1.5	.9
8	21	Machines............	3.022	5.5	5.2	82.0	3.5	3.8
9	18	Indefinite Titles	3.021	4.7	3.8	86.6	2.9	1.9
10	1	Vocations...........	3.020	3.9	3.7	88.3	2.5	1.6
11	30	School.............	3.016	3.2	2.4	91.8	1.2	1.5
12.5	23	Music...............	3.015	4.0	4.2	86.1	2.9	2.7
12.5	16	Home Life...........	3.015	3.8	2.5	90.0	2.4	1.3
14	19	Leisure Activities......	3.013	2.9	3.5	89.5	1.9	2.2
15	28	Pupil Employment.....	3.011	2.4	2.8	91.5	1.4	1.9
16	9	Current Events........	3.009	1.6	2.8	92.8	1.3	1.5
17	20	Literature...........	3.006	2.1	2.0	93.0	2.0	.9
18	12	Getting Rich.........	3.004	3.5	2.6	88.6	3.3	2.1
19	34	Sympathy...........	3.003	.7	1.8	95.6	.7	1.2
21	8	Famous People.......	3.002	2.6	3.0	89.0	3.2	2.1
21	25	People..............	3.002	2.6	1.7	91.7	1.5	2.5
21	36	Winning Prizes.......	3.002	.7	1.7	95.5	1.3	.8
23	3	Animals............	3.001	2.3	2.6	90.3	2.1	2.6
24	22	Modern Industries	2.996	3.0	1.4	90.4	3.3	1.9
25	15	Historic Events........	2.991	2.6	2.5	88.0	3.8	3.0
26	11	Fairy Tales..........	2.986	2.0	3.6	86.3	4.4	3.7
27	27	Proverbs............	2.982	1.6	1.5	90.6	3.0	3.3
28	4	Art.................	2.979	1.2	.7	92.3	2.4	3.4
29	7	Civics..............	2.970	.7	1.4	90.4	3.4	4.1
30	33	Social Problems.......	2.968	.4	1.2	91.0	4.4	3.0
31	31	Science.............	2.965	1.8	1.6	87.2	4.5	4.9
32	29	Religion............	2.955	.6	.5	89.6	4.7	4.5
33	14	Health..............	2.934	.9	.4	86.0	6.1	6.6
34	32	Sentiment...........	2.927	1.3	2.0	81.6	6.2	8.9
35	13	Handwork..........	2.925	1.2	1.4	83.8	6.3	7.4
36	6	Children............	2.917	.8	.8	82.8	6.6	8.8

Legend: B—5; NB—4; No Choice—3; NL—2; L—1.

TABLE XVI
Rank Order List of Composition Title Ratings by 1,199 Seventh Grade Boys

Rank	Title No.	Title	Median	Per Cent of Choices per Weight				
				5	4	3	2	1
1	9	Current Events	3.078	7.1	9.3	79.6	2.0	2.0
2	24	Outdoor Activities	3.071	7.8	5.4	85.5	.8	.4
3.5	2	Adventure	3.064	7.9	5.3	84.2	1.3	1.3
3.5	35	Travel	3.064	7.8	5.1	85.2	.8	1.2
5	3	Animals	3.057	7.1	5.5	84.3	2.0	1.1
6	8	Famous People	3.051	5.3	7.3	83.3	1.8	2.3
7	12	Getting Rich	3.042	7.6	4.6	82.3	2.2	3.3
8	19	Leisure Activities	3.034	5.4	3.8	87.3	1.4	2.0
9	5	Athletics	3.031	3.0	4.1	91.5	.9	.5
10	10	Ethics	3.030	3.3	3.8	91.1	1.2	.6
11	20	Literature	3.029	2.9	4.6	90.2	1.2	1.1
12	28	Pupil Employment	3.017	3.8	2.4	90.5	1.6	1.7
13	21	Machines	3.006	1.8	2.7	92.1	2.0	1.4
14.5	22	Modern Industries	3.002	2.8	1.3	92.1	2.3	1.5
14.5	34	Sympathy	3.002	.8	1.2	96.5	1.0	.6
16	17	Humorous Anecdotes	3.000	1.5	2.3	92.3	2.7	1.2
17	1	Vocations	2.999	1.6	1.6	93.3	1.8	1.8
18	26	Personal Experience	2.998	1.6	1.7	92.7	2.2	1.8
19	36	Winning Prizes	2.997	1.0	2.3	93.0	3.0	.8
20	16	Home Life	2.996	1.3	1.9	92.7	2.0	2.0
21	15	Historical Events	2.993	2.6	2.1	89.4	1.9	4.0
22	29	Religion	2.988	.6	.8	94.8	1.4	2.4
23	30	School	2.985	1.3	2.1	90.5	2.8	3.3
24	4	Art	2.984	.8	.7	93.8	3.1	1.6
25	31	Science	2.980	.7	1.7	91.6	3.6	2.5
26	7	Civics	2.978	.5	.5	93.8	3.2	2.0
27	11	Fairy Tales	2.975	.8	1.9	90.2	3.8	3.4
28	25	People	2.973	.9	1.4	90.4	3.8	3.5
29.5	13	Handwork	2.972	2.2	1.8	87.0	4.2	4.8
29.5	33	Social Problems	2.972	.5	1.0	91.8	2.9	3.8
31	23	Music	2.960	1.8	2.0	85.4	6.3	4.4
32	14	Health	2.959	.7	.4	90.3	4.3	4.2
33	18	Indefinite Titles	2.957	2.8	3.3	80.8	7.1	6.0
34	27	Proverbs	2.953	.3	.6	89.6	5.1	4.3
35	6	Children	2.916	.2	.5	84.3	5.9	9.1
36	32	Sentiment	2.908	.5	1.8	80.6	6.1	11.0

Legend: B—5; NB—4; No Choice—3; NL—2; L—1.

TABLE XVII
RANK ORDER LIST OF COMPOSITION TITLE RATINGS BY 1,205 EIGHTH GRADE BOYS

RANK	TITLE No.	TITLE	MEDIAN	PER CENT OF CHOICES PER WEIGHT				
				5	4	3	2	1
1	9	Current Events.........	3.091	9.2	8.0	80.1	1.3	1.2
2.5	2	Adventure.............	3.078	10.5	5.3	81.3	1.7	1.2
2.5	35	Travel................	3.078	8.3	6.2	84.1	1.0	.4
4	24	Outdoor Activities.....	3.068	7.6	5.5	85.5	.7	.7
5	5	Athletics..............	3.049	4.8	5.6	88.0	.8	.7
6.5	3	Animals...............	3.045	5.6	5.1	86.6	1.8	.9
6.5	10	Ethics................	3.045	4.7	5.1	88.6	.3	1.3
8	8	Famous People........	3.038	5.2	5.6	84.8	2.1	2.2
9	19	Leisure Activities......	3.030	4.0	5.1	87.6	1.8	1.7
10	20	Literature.............	3.022	2.6	3.7	91.5	1.5	.7
11	28	Pupil Employment.....	3.012	2.5	2.6	92.3	1.2	1.4
12	12	Getting Rich..........	3.011	4.0	4.1	85.9	3.3	2.7
13	1	Vocations.............	3.009	3.0	2.3	91.0	2.1	1.7
14	21	Machines.............	3.007	2.5	3.1	90.3	2.5	1.7
15.5	26	Personal Experience....	3.005	1.8	2.3	92.8	1.9	1.2
15.5	22	Modern Industries.....	3.005	2.6	1.7	92.6	1.7	1.5
17	15	Historic Events........	3.004	3.1	2.3	90.0	2.7	1.8
18	34	Sympathy.............	2.999	1.0	1.7	94.6	1.9	.8
19	36	Winning Prizes........	2.998	.7	2.7	92.6	2.1	1.8
20.5	17	Humorous Anecdotes...	2.992	.5	1.8	93.9	2.1	1.7
20.5	29	Religion..............	2.992	.7	1.0	95.2	1.4	1.7
22	16	Home Life............	2.988	1.2	1.2	93.2	2.9	1.6
23.5	7	Civics................	2.986	.6	1.3	93.6	2.2	2.3
23.5	31	Science...............	2.986	1.7	1.5	91.3	3.2	2.3
25	13	Handwork............	2.976	1.5	2.3	88.3	4.1	3.7
25	4	Art...................	2.974	.5	.6	93.3	3.1	2.7
27	14	Health................	2.960	.5	.6	90.7	3.4	4.8
28.5	18	Indefinite Titles.......	2.954	1.8	1.7	85.1	6.3	5.1
28.5	23	Music................	2.954	1.2	2.2	85.3	5.3	5.9
30	27	Proverbs.............	2.953	.7	1.1	88.2	5.5	4.5
31	11	Fairy Tales...........	2.951	1.0	1.2	87.5	5.5	5.0
32	33	Social Problems........	2.947	.7	.6	88.3	4.5	6.0
33	25	People................	2.932	1.1	1.6	90.7	3.2	3.5
34	6	Children..............	2.930	.5	1.0	85.1	5.8	7.6
35	30	School................	2.928	1.0	1.3	89.4	3.6	4.6
36	32	Sentiment.............	2.903	.3	.8	82.3	5.6	11.0

Legend: B—5; NB—4; No Choice—3; NL—2; L—1.

TABLE XVIII
Rank Order List of Composition Title Ratings by 1,427 Ninth Grade Boys

Rank	Title No.	Title	Median	Per Cent of Choices per Weight				
				5	4	3	2	1
1	35	Travel................	3.070	8.3	5.3	84.8	.9	.8
2	24	Outdoor Activities......	3.066	7.5	5.3	85.0	1.0	.4
3	2	Adventure.............	3.060	7.8	4.8	85.0	1.5	.8
4	5	Athletics..............	3.055	5.8	5.0	88.0	.7	.5
5	8	Famous People.........	3.044	4.9	5.9	86.0	1.8	1.5
6	9	Current Events.........	3.037	4.6	6.4	84.2	1.9	2.9
7	10	Ethics................	3.032	2.8	4.6	91.0	.8	.7
8.5	3	Animals...............	3.030	4.6	4.5	87.1	1.7	2.2
8.5	21	Machines..............	3.030	3.8	3.9	90.2	1.7	.6
10	19	Leisure Activities......	3.026	4.0	3.6	89.6	1.3	1.5
11	28	Pupil Employment.....	3.021	3.3	2.7	91.8	1.5	.8
12.5	12	Getting Rich..........	3.012	3.6	3.4	88.2	2.3	2.6
12.5	20	Literature.............	3.012	2.4	2.2	93.1	1.1	1.2
14	15	Historic Events........	3.006	3.6	2.7	88.5	3.0	2.2
15	22	Modern Industries......	3.004	2.2	2.4	91.5	2.5	1.4
16	34	Sympathy.............	3.003	.8	1.3	96.4	1.0	.5
17.5	17	Humorous Anecdotes...	3.002	1.8	3.1	90.5	2.4	2.2
17.5	26	Personal Experience....	3.002	2.1	2.6	90.8	1.9	2.6
19.5	36	Winning Prizes........	2.998	.8	2.4	93.4	2.0	1.4
19.5	1	Vocations.............	2.998	2.7	2.3	89.6	3.2	2.2
21	16	Home Life............	2.994	1.5	1.1	93.7	2.0	1.7
22	25	People................	2.985	1.0	1.3	92.8	2.7	2.3
23	30	School................	2.984	2.1	2.0	89.0	3.4	3.5
24	27	Proverbs..............	2.982	.9	1.3	91.0	4.3	2.5
25.5	7	Civics................	2.981	1.1	1.1	92.1	2.3	3.4
25.5	14	Health................	2.981	1.8	1.1	91.0	2.6	3.6
27	18	Indefinite Titles.......	2.979	2.9	3.0	84.5	4.8	4.8
28	29	Religion..............	2.978	.4	.7	93.7	2.5	2.7
29	31	Science...............	2.976	1.3	1.4	92.1	2.8	2.6
30	4	Art...................	2.975	.5	.6	93.1	3.1	2.7
31	33	Social Problems........	2.969	1.2	1.3	89.6	4.4	3.6
32	13	Handwork............	2.967	2.5	2.1	85.3	4.8	5.5
33	23	Music................	2.954	1.7	2.5	84.2	5.0	6.7
34	11	Fairy Tales...........	2.952	1.1	1.5	86.5	5.0	5.8
35	32	Sentiment............	2.911	.2	1.2	82.6	6.6	9.5
36	6	Children.............	2.909	.3	.9	83.8	6.9	8.2

Legend: B—5; NB—4; No Choice—3; NL—2; L—1.

TABLE XIX
Rank Order List of Composition Title Ratings by 2,311 Tenth Grade Boys

Rank	Title No.	Title	Median	Per Cent of Choices per Weight				
				5	4	3	2	1
1	5	Athletics	3.072	6.9	6.4	85.5	.7	.5
2	35	Travel	3.052	6.2	4.7	87.2	1.3	.6
3	24	Outdoor Activities	3.050	5.6	4.6	88.4	.9	.6
4	2	Adventure	3.045	5.5	3.7	89.5	.7	.6
5	10	Ethics	3.038	3.2	4.4	91.7	.4	.3
6	9	Current Events	3.032	3.4	5.2	88.5	1.6	1.4
7	21	Machines	3.026	4.5	3.5	88.5	2.1	1.3
8.5	8	Famous People	3.020	3.9	5.0	85.5	2.5	3.0
8.5	19	Leisure Activities	3.020	3.9	3.0	89.8	1.8	1.5
10	20	Literature	3.019	2.9	3.0	91.7	1.1	1.3
11	28	Pupil Employment	3.016	2.2	2.2	94.1	.9	.5
12.5	1	Vocations	3.014	3.7	2.6	90.0	1.9	1.8
12.5	3	Animals	3.014	2.0	4.4	89.6	1.8	2.2
14	30	School	3.004	3.0	1.9	90.8	2.2	2.1
16	12	Getting Rich	3.002	2.7	3.4	88.3	2.8	2.9
16	22	Modern Industries	3.002	2.6	1.3	92.6	2.3	1.2
16	34	Sympathy	3.002	.9	1.4	95.6	1.2	.9
18	16	Home Life	3.001	1.8	1.6	93.3	1.9	1.4
19.5	17	Humorous Anecdotes	2.999	1.3	2.2	92.8	1.9	1.8
19.5	26	Personal Experience	2.999	1.6	1.9	93.0	1.9	1.8
21	18	Indefinite Titles	2.998	2.9	2.8	88.3	3.2	2.9
22	36	Winning Prizes	2.997	1.2	1.8	93.3	2.2	1.5
23	25	People	2.996	1.4	1.7	92.9	2.4	1.6
24	31	Science	2.992	1.7	1.9	91.3	2.5	2.6
25	4	Art	2.985	.4	1.2	93.9	2.4	2.0
26	15	Historic Events	2.984	2.2	2.1	88.9	3.5	3.4
27	7	Civics	2.983	1.0	.9	92.9	2.5	2.6
28	33	Social Problems	2.981	.7	1.0	93.0	2.4	2.9
29	29	Religion	2.977	.4	.5	94.0	2.1	3.1
30.5	23	Music	2.975	2.7	2.4	85.4	4.7	4.7
30.5	27	Proverbs	2.975	.4	1.1	92.5	3.4	2.7
32	13	Handwork	2.972	2.6	1.9	86.2	4.2	5.0
33	14	Health	2.963	.8	.9	90.2	4.2	4.0
34	11	Fairy Tales	2.940	1.0	1.4	84.9	6.3	6.4
35	6	Children	2.927	.3	.7	85.7	6.4	7.0
36	32	Sentiment	2.919	.6	1.1	83.1	5.4	9.9

Legend: B—5; NB—4; No Choice—3; NL—2; L—1.

TABLE XX
Rank Order List of Composition Title Ratings by 625 Eleventh Grade Boys

Rank	Title No.	Title	Median	Per Cent of Choices per Weight				
				5	4	3	2	1
1	5	Athletics	3.108	9.9	9.3	78.7	1.1	1.0
2	21	Machines	3.072	9.6	4.5	83.7	1.1	1.0
3	35	Travel	3.068	5.9	8.3	82.9	1.9	1.0
4	24	Outdoor Activities	3.054	6.1	5.6	86.6	.3	1.4
5	2	Adventure	3.031	4.5	3.6	89.5	.6	1.8
6	1	Vocations	3.028	5.0	4.0	87.0	1.4	2.6
7.5	20	Literature	3.022	3.7	2.2	92.3	1.0	.8
7.5	9	Current Events	3.022	2.4	5.0	89.3	.8	2.6
9	10	Ethics	3.019	1.8	3.7	92.8	1.0	.8
11.5	19	Leisure Activities	3.016	3.8	3.5	88.2	1.9	2.6
11.5	28	Pupil Employment	3.016	1.9	2.6	94.2	1.1	.2
11.5	30	School	3.016	3.2	2.6	91.7	1.4	1.1
11.5	22	Modern Industries	3.016	3.0	3.4	90.2	1.4	1.9
14.5	8	Famous People	3.008	4.8	4.2	83.5	3.6	4.0
14.5	16	Home Life	3.008	2.2	2.4	92.3	1.4	1.6
16	12	Getting Rich	3.007	3.8	4.8	84.0	3.8	3.6
17.5	17	Humorous Anecdotes	3.001	1.3	2.9	91.9	2.7	1.3
17.5	34	Sympathy	3.001	.6	1.0	97.1	1.0	.3
19	3	Animals	3.000	1.8	2.7	91.2	2.4	1.9
20.5	18	Indefinite Titles	2.999	2.9	2.9	88.5	3.4	2.4
20.5	26	Personal Experience	2.999	1.9	1.6	93.0	2.1	1.4
22	25	People	2.995	2.4	1.9	90.6	3.2	1.9
23	31	Science	2.990	2.7	1.4	90.1	3.2	2.6
24	15	Historic Events	2.988	3.7	1.3	88.2	3.0	3.8
25	4	Art	2.987	1.0	.8	94.2	1.9	2.1
26	23	Music	2.978	2.2	2.4	90.1	3.2	2.1
27	29	Religion	2.975	1.0	.5	92.7	2.6	3.4
28	36	Winning Prizes	2.973	.8	1.6	93.5	1.9	2.2
29	7	Civics	2.967	.6	1.8	89.5	3.8	4.3
30	27	Proverbs	2.965	.6	.6	91.2	3.7	3.8
31	33	Social Problems	2.964	1.3	.5	90.1	4.8	3.4
32	14	Health	2.956	.5	.8	89.6	4.8	4.3
33	13	Handwork	2.946	1.0	1.6	85.8	5.3	6.4
34	11	Fairy Tales	2.937	1.1	2.1	83.2	4.8	8.8
35	32	Sentiment	2.901	.3	1.3	81.0	9.0	8.5
36	6	Children	2.900	.3	1.0	81.5	9.4	7.8

Legend: B—5; NB—4; No Choice—3; NL—2; L—1.

TABLE XXI
Rank Order List of Composition Title Ratings by 542 Twelfth Grade Boys

Rank	Title No.	Title	Median	Per Cent of Choices per Weight				
				5	4	3	2	1
1	5	Athletics	3.082	8.7	6.3	83.8	.7	.6
2	35	Travel	3.080	7.4	7.0	84.7	.4	.6
3	21	Machines	3.076	7.6	7.4	82.5	1.1	1.5
4	24	Outdoor Activities	3.056	5.0	6.3	87.3	.9	.6
5	28	Pupil Employment	3.036	3.7	4.4	90.3	.7	.9
6	1	Vocations	3.033	5.4	4.4	86.2	2.8	1.3
7	10	Ethics	3.031	3.3	3.7	91.7	.4	.9
8	26	Personal Experience	3.030	2.2	5.4	90.3	1.5	.7
9	2	Adventure	3.029	5.2	3.9	88.8	.7	1.5
10	19	Leisure Activities	3.026	4.1	4.2	88.0	1.7	2.1
11	9	Current Events	3.019	2.4	3.1	92.5	1.1	.9
12.5	17	Humorous Anecdotes	3.016	3.3	2.8	90.8	1.7	1.5
12.5	22	Modern Industries	3.016	4.2	1.8	90.8	2.1	1.1
14	30	School	3.011	3.1	1.8	92.1	1.5	1.5
16	8	Famous People	3.009	2.8	4.2	87.1	3.5	2.4
16	18	Indefinite Titles	3.009	3.9	2.6	88.6	3.7	1.3
16	23	Music	3.009	4.1	3.7	86.0	3.0	3.3
18	25	People	3.004	3.0	1.1	92.7	1.3	2.1
19	16	Home Life	3.002	2.4	1.7	92.3	1.8	1.8
20	36	Winning Prizes	3.000	.6	1.1	96.7	.6	1.1
21	20	Literature	2.999	1.7	1.5	93.5	2.1	1.3
22	34	Sympathy	2.998	.2	1.3	96.7	1.1	.7
23.5	3	Animals	2.996	1.7	3.0	90.0	2.1	3.3
23.5	12	Getting Rich	2.996	3.1	2.6	87.7	4.4	2.1
25	15	Historic Events	2.982	2.2	1.8	88.8	4.1	3.1
26	7	Civics	2.980	.7	1.7	91.5	2.4	3.7
27.5	4	Art	2.976	.7	.7	92.7	3.0	3.0
27.5	31	Science	2.976	2.6	1.8	86.9	3.5	5.2
29	27	Proverbs	2.964	.9	1.3	89.2	4.4	4.2
30	33	Social Problems	2.961	.0	.7	91.4	4.6	3.3
31	29	Religion	2.956	.2	.4	91.0	4.4	4.1
32	14	Health	2.953	1.1	.7	88.0	4.6	5.5
33	11	Fairy Tales	2.948	.7	2.1	85.6	6.1	5.5
34	13	Handwork	2.941	1.3	1.8	84.2	6.1	6.8
35	32	Sentiment	2.900	.6	1.5	80.0	7.2	10.9
36	6	Children	2.886	.4	.6	80.0	9.0	10.1

Legend: B—5; NB—4; No Choice—3; NL—2; L—1.

TABLE XXII
Rank Order List of Composition Title Ratings by 1,320 Seventh Grade Girls

Rank	Title No.	Title	Median	Per Cent of Choices per Weight				
				5	4	3	2	1
1	35	Travel................	3.094	11.6	5.7	80.7	.8	1.2
2	2	Adventure............	3.067	9.3	4.7	83.0	1.6	1.4
3	3	Animals..............	3.050	5.2	5.5	87.5	1.0	.9
4	12	Getting Rich..........	3.048	7.2	5.0	83.7	1.7	2.5
5	20	Literature............	3.041	3.9	5.1	89.2	.8	1.0
6.5	19	Leisure Activities	3.038	4.1	5.3	87.9	1.0	1.7
6.5	24	Outdoor Activities	3.038	4.8	3.9	89.3	1.1	.8
8	26	Personal Experience....	3.032	5.4	4.3	86.2	2.6	1.6
9	10	Ethics................	3.026	3.2	2.8	92.9	.5	.6
10	29	Religion..............	3.024	3.6	2.7	91.7	1.1	.8
11	17	Humorous Anecdotes...	3.018	2.1	3.8	91.4	1.2	1.4
12	34	Sympathy.............	3.014	1.7	2.7	93.9	.8	1.0
13	16	Home Life............	3.013	3.8	3.6	87.7	2.4	2.6
14	28	Pupil Employment.....	3.011	2.4	2.5	92.2	1.0	1.9
15	6	Children..............	3.004	3.5	4.1	85.5	4.2	2.7
16	30	School................	3.000	2.9	2.7	88.9	2.5	3.0
17	36	Winning Prizes........	2.998	.5	2.8	93.1	1.7	2.0
18	8	Famous People........	2.996	1.7	2.3	91.3	2.2	2.5
19.5	1	Vocations.............	2.994	1.7	1.4	92.6	2.0	2.3
19.5	4	Art...................	2.994	1.2	1.1	94.2	1.6	1.9
21	5	Athletics.............	2.992	.4	1.1	95.6	1.4	1.5
22.5	9	Current Events........	2.988	2.1	3.2	86.9	3.6	4.2
22.5	11	Fairy Tales...........	2.988	2.4	2.1	88.8	3.4	3.3
24	27	Proverbs..............	2.984	1.5	2.7	88.8	4.1	2.9
25.5	13	Handwork............	2.981	.7	1.2	92.6	2.8	2.7
25.5	18	Indefinite Titles	2.981	2.7	3.6	84.3	5.2	4.2
27	23	Music................	2.977	1.7	2.6	87.3	4.0	4.3
28	15	Historical Events.......	2.970	2.4	1.5	87.0	4.3	4.7
29	7	Civics................	2.968	.0	.6	92.8	3.8	2.8
30	22	Industries............	2.963	.8	1.0	91.6	3.6	3.0
31	25	People................	2.959	.6	.9	89.6	3.8	5.1
32	32	Sentiment............	2.958	1.7	2.9	83.9	5.3	6.3
33	31	Science...............	2.955	.5	2.1	87.0	5.7	4.7
34	14	Health................	2.950	1.0	.4	88.4	4.9	5.3
35	33	Social Problems........	2.946	.8	1.7	88.5	5.0	3.9
36	21	Machines.............	2.928	.2	.2	86.8	6.5	6.3

Legend: B—5; NB—4; No Choice—3; NL—2; L—1.

TABLE XXIII
Rank Order List of Composition Title Ratings by 1,335 Eighth Grade Girls

Rank	Title No.	Title	Median	Per Cent of Choices per Weight				
				5	4	3	2	1
1	35	Travel...............	3.126	13.9	7.8	75.5	1.4	1.3
2	2	Adventure............	3.062	8.6	4.3	84.5	1.5	1.0
3	12	Getting Rich..........	3.047	6.1	6.0	83.5	2.0	2.4
4	24	Outdoor Activities.....	3.040	4.6	4.5	89.0	1.1	.9
5.5	10	Ethics...............	3.036	4.0	4.1	90.2	.9	.7
5.5	20	Literature............	3.036	3.2	4.9	90.2	.7	1.0
7	3	Animals..............	3.035	4.0	5.2	87.5	1.6	1.6
8	19	Leisure Activities......	3.031	4.0	4.5	88.6	1.6	1.4
9	26	Personal Experience....	3.030	4.3	4.8	87.0	2.7	1.3
10	34	Sympathy.............	3.017	2.2	2.5	93.5	.8	.9
11.5	16	Home Life............	3.016	4.1	2.5	89.6	1.9	1.9
11.5	29	Religion..............	3.016	3.4	2.5	91.2	1.3	1.6
13	28	Pupil Employment.....	3.011	2.1	2.3	93.1	1.2	1.3
14	17	Humorous Anecdotes...	3.010	2.2	3.7	90.0	2.7	1.4
15	9	Current Events........	3.008	3.4	3.2	88.2	3.1	2.0
16	30	School...............	3.006	3.4	2.6	89.1	2.0	2.9
17.5	1	Vocations............	3.001	2.1	2.9	90.0	2.5	2.4
17.5	5	Athletics.............	3.001	1.1	1.7	94.5	1.5	1.2
19	8	Famous People........	2.997	2.8	2.2	89.2	2.5	3.1
20	36	Winning Prizes........	2.992	.9	1.6	93.3	2.4	1.7
21	4	Art..................	2.990	.9	.9	94.6	1.9	1.7
22	23	Music................	2.989	1.7	4.1	85.8	3.4	4.9
23	32	Sentiment............	2.986	1.6	3.4	85.5	3.3	6.2
24	11	Fairy Tales...........	2.982	2.1	1.6	89.3	3.5	3.5
25	22	Modern Industries.....	2.981	.7	1.5	92.1	3.4	2.4
26	18	Indefinite Titles.......	2.979	2.2	3.7	85.6	4.9	4.1
27	15	Historic Events........	2.977	1.9	2.1	87.9	4.3	3.7
28	27	Proverbs.............	2.975	1.0	1.9	89.7	4.7	2.7
29	6	Children.............	2.972	2.2	2.1	86.6	4.6	4.5
30	13	Handwork............	2.971	.6	1.0	91.6	3.0	3.9
31	7	Civics................	2.969	.4	.6	92.5	3.4	3.1
32.5	33	Social Problems........	2.964	1.0	1.1	89.2	4.3	4.3
32.5	25	People...............	2.964	.6	.4	90.6	4.6	3.7
34	31	Science...............	2.956	1.0	.7	88.6	4.6	5.1
35	14	Health...............	2.955	1.3	1.4	86.9	4.7	5.7
36	21	Machines.............	2.928	.4	.3	86.2	5.5	7.7

Legend: B—5; NB—4; No Choice—3; NL—2; L—1.

TABLE XXIV
Rank Order List of Composition Title Ratings by 1,355 Ninth Grade Girls

Rank	Title No.	Title	Median	Per Cent of Choices per Weight				
				5	4	3	2	1
1	35	Travel...............	3.103	9.6	8.5	80.4	1.0	.6
2	2	Adventure............	3.057	7.4	4.6	85.8	1.3	1.0
3	26	Personal Experience....	3.048	5.6	5.5	86.0	1.3	1.7
4	10	Ethics................	3.047	4.9	4.4	89.7	.7	.3
5.5	19	Leisure Activities......	3.040	4.3	4.9	88.5	1.0	1.3
5.5	24	Outdoor Activities......	3.040	4.6	3.8	90.4	.8	.4
7	20	Literature.............	3.037	3.9	4.6	89.4	1.2	.8
8	3	Animals..............	3.028	3.6	3.7	90.3	1.3	1.1
9	16	Home Life............	3.020	3.7	3.2	89.7	2.2	1.2
10	12	Getting Rich..........	3.019	3.2	5.3	86.3	2.4	2.9
11.5	17	Humorous Anecdotes...	3.018	2.1	4.6	90.0	1.9	1.5
11.5	34	Sympathy.............	3.018	1.9	2.8	94.0	.9	.5
13	30	School................	3.014	4.3	2.5	89.0	1.8	2.5
14	29	Religion..............	3.013	3.0	2.2	92.0	1.6	1.2
15	8	Famous People........	3.011	3.9	2.7	88.7	2.3	2.4
16	28	Pupil Employment.....	3.006	2.0	1.6	94.2	1.7	.6
17	5	Athletics.............	3.003	1.2	1.6	95.2	1.1	1.0
18	9	Current Events........	3.001	2.4	3.0	89.2	3.5	1.8
19	36	Winning Prizes........	2.994	.7	1.4	94.6	1.6	1.7
20	4	Art...................	2.993	1.0	1.6	93.6	2.0	1.8
21.5	18	Indefinite Titles.......	2.992	2.3	2.7	88.6	4.4	2.0
21.5	27	Proverbs..............	2.992	1.4	2.8	90.1	2.7	3.0
23	1	Vocations.............	2.991	2.1	1.8	90.4	2.7	2.9
24	23	Music.................	2.984	1.8	2.7	88.2	3.8	3.5
25	15	Historic Events........	2.980	3.4	2.6	84.6	4.1	5.3
26	14	Health................	2.976	2.0	5.7	80.7	5.0	6.6
27	6	Children..............	2.974	1.3	1.8	89.1	3.6	4.2
28	33	Social Problems........	2.972	1.5	1.2	89.8	3.4	4.2
29.5	11	Fairy Tales............	2.971	2.3	1.8	86.7	5.0	4.1
29.5	32	Sentiment.............	2.971	1.5	2.7	86.6	3.6	5.6
31	25	People................	2.965	.7	1.0	90.2	4.3	3.8
32	7	Civics................	2.963	1.0	1.0	89.3	3.6	5.0
33	13	Handwork.............	2.961	1.5	1.3	87.6	4.4	5.2
34	22	Modern Industries......	2.959	1.7	.8	89.3	3.7	4.4
35	31	Science	2.944	1.4	.7	86.2	6.0	5.7
36	21	Machines.............	2.923	.1	.9	85.0	6.4	7.6

Legend: B—5; NB—4; No Choice—3; NL—2; L—1.

TABLE XXV
Rank Order List of Composition Title Ratings by 2,109 Tenth Grade Girls

Rank	Title No.	Title	Median	Per Cent of Choices per Weight				
				5	4	3	2	1
1	35	Travel.................	3.106	10.6	7.9	79.8	.4	1.2
2	2	Adventure.............	3.049	6.6	3.8	87.7	.7	1.1
3	26	Personal Experience.....	3.047	5.9	4.8	86.8	1.5	1.1
4	24	Outdoor Activities	3.042	4.9	4.5	88.8	1.2	.6
5	10	Ethics.................	3.036	4.1	3.4	91.6	.7	.2
6	20	Literature.............	3.035	3.8	4.1	90.5	.9	.8
7	17	Humorous Anecdotes...	3.034	2.7	6.2	88.3	1.7	1.2
8	18	Indefinite Titles	3.027	4.0	4.6	87.7	2.0	1.7
9	19	Leisure Activities......	3.026	3.4	4.3	89.4	1.4	1.5
10	30	School................	3.023	4.8	2.6	89.5	1.9	1.2
11	34	Sympathy.............	3.020	2.2	3.2	92.7	.9	.9
12	5	Athletics..............	3.013	1.9	2.1	94.4	1.1	.5
13.5	3	Animals...............	3.010	2.2	2.7	92.0	1.9	1.2
13.5	12	Getting Rich..........	3.010	2.6	3.9	88.8	2.4	2.4
15.5	1	Vocations.............	3.009	3.9	3.0	87.6	2.6	2.8
15.5	16	Home Life	3.009	3.2	2.5	90.5	2.6	1.4
17	27	Proverbs..............	3.005	1.8	3.1	91.2	2.3	1.6
18	28	Pupil Employment.....	3.001	1.3	1.3	95.0	1.4	.9
20	29	Religion...............	2.998	1.4	1.3	94.3	1.1	2.0
20	36	Winning Prizes........	2.998	.8	1.4	95.1	1.7	1.0
20	4	Art...................	2.998	1.2	1.9	93.6	1.6	1.8
22	23	Music.................	2.997	2.3	3.5	87.6	4.0	2.5
23	8	Famous People........	2.991	1.5	1.8	91.9	2.6	2.3
24	33	Social Problems........	2.985	1.7	1.1	91.6	2.8	2.7
25	25	People................	2.979	.9	.8	92.7	2.9	2.6
26	6	Children..............	2.978	1.7	1.3	90.0	3.2	3.7
27	9	Current Events........	2.970	.7	1.4	90.6	3.7	3.6
28	11	Fairy Tales............	2.969	1.3	1.4	90.0	4.0	3.4
29	22	Modern Industries	2.968	1.1	.5	91.0	3.6	3.8
30	32	Sentiment.............	2.963	.9	1.8	88.3	4.0	5.0
31	15	Historic Events........	2.961	2.3	2.6	83.8	5.0	6.3
32	7	Civics.................	2.954	.7	.9	88.7	4.8	4.9
33	14	Health................	2.952	1.8	1.0	86.1	5.5	5.6
34	31	Science................	2.948	1.4	.9	86.7	4.2	6.8
35	13	Handwork.............	2.946	.6	.9	87.7	4.9	5.9
36	21	Machines..............	2.933	.6	.7	86.1	5.6	6.9

Legend: B—5; NB—4; No Choice—3; NL—2; L—1.

TABLE XXVI
Rank Order List of Composition Title Ratings by 707 Eleventh Grade Girls

Rank	Title No.	Title	Median	Per Cent of Choices per Weight				
				5	4	3	2	1
1	35	Travel	3.123	13.6	6.6	78.8	.4	.6
2	26	Personal Experience	3.056	5.5	6.4	85.7	1.1	1.3
3	2	Adventure	3.044	5.5	4.5	87.6	1.6	.8
4	24	Outdoor Activities	3.040	4.2	5.1	88.2	1.4	1.0
5	5	Athletics	3.035	2.7	4.8	91.3	.8	.4
6	30	School	3.034	5.4	3.5	88.1	1.7	1.3
7	10	Ethics	3.033	3.5	3.5	91.8	.3	.8
8.5	18	Indefinite Titles	3.032	4.0	4.8	88.0	2.3	1.0
8.5	20	Literature	3.032	3.4	3.8	91.3	.8	.7
10	16	Home Life	3.031	5.8	3.0	87.6	2.7	1.0
11.5	3	Animals	3.030	4.2	3.1	91.0	1.0	.8
11.5	17	Humorous Anecdotes	3.030	3.3	5.1	88.5	1.6	1.7
13	34	Sympathy	3.025	2.5	3.1	93.2	.4	.7
14	19	Leisure Activities	3.020	3.5	3.0	90.4	1.6	1.6
15	12	Getting Rich	3.010	2.8	3.0	90.0	1.8	2.4
16.5	15	Historic Events	3.001	3.3	3.8	85.9	3.5	3.5
16.5	27	Proverbs	3.001	2.5	2.0	91.0	2.8	1.7
18	28	Pupil Employment	3.000	.7	2.0	94.5	.8	2.0
19	8	Famous People	2.998	1.8	2.3	91.3	1.1	3.5
20	11	Fairy Tales	2.994	3.8	2.5	86.2	3.4	4.1
22	1	Vocations	2.992	2.4	2.3	89.1	3.3	3.0
22	23	Music	2.992	1.7	3.3	88.6	3.7	2.8
22	36	Winning Prizes	2.992	.4	1.6	94.4	1.7	2.0
24	25	People	2.991	1.0	2.0	92.2	2.4	2.4
25	9	Current Events	2.988	.3	3.1	91.0	4.0	1.7
26	4	Art	2.987	1.4	1.6	91.5	3.1	2.4
27	29	Religion	2.974	1.0	.3	92.5	3.0	3.3
28	6	Children	2.970	.7	1.7	89.7	3.1	4.8
29	33	Social Problems	2.968	1.7	1.1	88.6	2.8	5.8
30	22	Modern Industries	2.957	.6	1.6	88.0	4.2	5.7
31	7	Civics	2.950	.8	1.1	87.1	6.2	4.7
32	32	Sentiment	2.948	.7	1.3	86.8	5.1	6.1
33	31	Science	2.945	.7	.6	87.9	5.8	5.1
34	13	Handwork	2.938	1.8	.8	84.0	7.4	5.9
35	14	Health	2.935	2.0	1.3	82.6	6.6	7.5
36	21	Machines	2.932	.7	.7	85.5	6.5	6.6

Legend: B—5; NB—4; No Choice—3; NL—2; L—1.

TABLE XXVII

RANK ORDER LIST OF COMPOSITION TITLE RATINGS BY 410 TWELFTH GRADE GIRLS

Rank	Title No.	Title	Median	Per Cent of Choices per Weight					
				5	4	3	2	1
1	35	Travel...............	3.125	10.2	10.5	78.0	.7	.5
2	26	Personal Experience	3.055	6.1	5.4	86.6	.7	1.2
3	5	Athletics.............	3.040	4.6	3.9	90.0	1.2	.2
4	18	Indefinite Titles........	3.039	5.9	5.4	84.1	2.0	2.7
5	11	Fairy Tales...........	3.034	3.6	5.6	87.3	2.2	1.2
6.5	16	Home Life............	3.032	5.6	3.6	87.1	3.1	.5
6.5	17	Humorous Anecdotes...	3.032	2.2	5.1	91.2	1.2	.2
8	10	Ethics................	3.031	3.4	4.1	90.5	.7	1.2
9	2	Adventure............	3.030	4.4	3.9	88.8	1.2	1.7
10	24	Outdoor Activities......	3.028	4.6	1.7	92.5	.7	.5
11	30	School...............	3.023	3.1	3.1	91.5	.7	1.4
12	23	Music................	3.022	3.9	4.9	86.3	2.9	2.0
13	20	Literature............	3.016	2.7	2.7	92.2	2.0	.5
14	12	Getting Rich..........	3.015	3.9	2.7	89.5	1.7	2.2
15	34	Sympathy............	3.010	1.4	2.4	94.2	.2	1.7
16	3	Animals..............	3.008	3.1	2.2	90.7	2.2	1.7
17	27	Proverbs.............	3.005	2.4	1.7	92.7	1.2	2.0
18	36	Winning Prizes........	3.004	1.0	2.4	94.0	2.2	.5
19	1	Vocations............	3.003	2.0	2.7	91.2	2.2	2.0
20	15	Historic Events........	3.002	3.1	3.4	87.1	3.4	2.9
21	25	People...............	2.999	2.2	2.4	90.5	1.7	3.1
22	8	Famous People........	2.997	2.4	1.4	91.7	2.7	1.7
23.5	9	Current Events........	2.996	.5	2.4	93.4	1.4	2.2
23.5	19	Leisure Activities......	2.996	1.4	2.4	91.5	2.2	2.4
25	4	Art..................	2.983	1.7	.7	92.0	1.7	3.9
26	28	Pupil Employment.....	2.979	.7	.7	93.2	2.2	3.1
27	33	Social Problems........	2.977	1.0	1.7	90.5	4.1	2.7
28	22	Modern Industries	2.969	1.4	.7	90.0	4.9	2.9
29	32	Sentiment............	2.962	2.2	2.7	83.9	4.9	6.3
30	7	Civics................	2.958	.7	1.0	89.0	4.6	4.6
31	6	Children..............	2.955	1.4	1.2	86.8	3.4	7.1
32	29	Religion..............	2.953	1.2	.7	87.8	5.1	5.1
33	31	Science...............	2.948	.7	1.2	87.4	5.9	4.9
34	21	Machines.............	2.943	2.7	2.4	81.5	6.6	6.8
35	13	Handwork............	2.921	1.0	.7	83.4	6.8	8.0
36	14	Health...............	2.908	.7	.0	83.2	8.0	8.0

Legend: B—5; NB—4; No Choice—3; NL—2; L—1.

The Reliability of the A, B, and C Lists of Composition Titles

Since Tables X to XXVII are based upon summations of the responses on all three lists of titles, it is necessary to note the degree of consistency between the three possible pairs of lists.

Perfect reliability could not be anticipated, for it would not be expected that each pupil would write each week for three weeks (three assignments) upon some phase of the same topic. He would be more likely, because of the method used, to indicate more consistency in his dislikes than in his three choices of topics for his three compositions. Nevertheless, some degree of consistency between results on the separate lists was needed as a basis for finding common interests. For this purpose, coefficients of correlation for all possible combinations of the three lists were worked out for the tenth grade. This grade was selected because it is representative of all five school systems participating, and the lists were used by a larger number of pupils in this grade than in any other. An average of 770 boys and 703 girls—a total of 1,473 pupils—used each list. The correlations in Table XXVIII were found by the rank-difference method.

TABLE XXVIII

RANK-DIFFERENCE COEFFICIENTS OF CORRELATION FOR THE THREE POSSIBLE PAIRS OF COMBINATIONS OF THE A, B, AND C LISTS

Data Obtained for Boys and for Girls in the Tenth Grade

Lists Correlated	Correlation Coefficients	
	Boys	Girls
AB	.58	.74
AC	.50	.62
BC	.34	.65

According to these coefficients a marked relationship exists among the lists.

The Reliability of the Rank Order Lists of Interests

If the rank order lists in Tables X to XXVII are true pictures of the interests of boys and girls in grades seven through twelve, it would be expected that the least variation between two lists would occur in adjacent grades; similarly, the greatest variation would be

48 *Written Composition Interests of High School Pupils*

between the most widely separated grades. These expectations are based on the assumption that there is some overlapping of ages from grade to grade and that changes in interest are therefore likely to vary least between adjacent grades. That these lists do indicate this type of variation is demonstrated by the correlations in Table XXIX. These Pearson product-moment coefficients of correlation were obtained by correlating the seventh grade lists with each of the other grade lists for boys, for girls, and for boys and girls together.

TABLE XXIX

CORRELATIONS OF THE RANK ORDER LISTS BETWEEN GRADE SEVEN AND EACH OF THE OTHER GRADES

GRADES CORRELATED	CORRELATION COEFFICIENTS		
	BOYS	GIRLS	BOYS AND GIRLS
7—8	.97	.94	.96
7—9	.95	.95	.94
7—10	.87	.83	.85
7—11	.76	.72	.81
7—12	.74	.66	.69

The various lists were subjected to another test of reliability. If the responses for any one list had occurred in a pure chance arrangement, it would be expected that 1/36 of all choices would occur under each of the ratings—B, NB, NL, and L—and that 32/36 of the choices would fall in the middle, or non-rated, class. In per cents, we would expect 2.78 per cent of the total choices to occur under each one of the four possible ratings. Kelley[2] gives a formula $\left(\sigma_p = \sqrt{\dfrac{pq}{N}}\right)$ which would enable one to determine the range within which a percentage should fall by chance. The specific problem is whether or not the data show a sufficiently marked divergence to be real, that is, whether or not the total per cent of ratings (of liking or disliking) for each category falls outside the limits of pure chance. Accordingly, the B and NB per cents for each title were combined and the NL and L ratings were totaled similarly. By chance the total of either of these two pairs would be $5.56 \pm 3\sigma$. A title was discarded from some considerations when both totals were found

[2] Kelley, Truman L., *Statistical Method*, p. 90. The Macmillan Company, New York, 1924.

Composition Interests Shown by Pupils' Choices

TABLE XXX
Categories of Interest Discarded Because of the Chance Character of the Data

Group	Grade					
	7	8	9	10	11	12
Boys	22 Mod. Ind. 17 Hum. Anecd. 15 Hist. Events	1 Vocations 21 Machines 15 Hist. Events	12 Getting Rich 15 Hist. Events 22 Mod. Ind. 17 Hum. Anecd. 26 Per. Exp. 1 Vocations 30 School	30 School 12 Getting Rich 18 Ind. Titles 15 Hist. Events	26 Per. Exp. 16 Home Life 19 Leisure Act. 17 Hum. Anecd. 18 Ind. Titles 3 Animals 9 Cur. Events 22 Mod. Ind. 25 People 31 Science 15 Hist. Events 23 Music	19 Leisure Act. 17 Hum. Anecd. 22 Mod. Ind. 30 School 8 Fam. People 18 Ind. Titles 23 Music 25 People 16 Home Life 20 Literature 3 Animals 12 Getting Rich 15 Hist. Events
Girls	16 Home Life 30 School 8 Fam. People 11 Fairy Tales 27 Proverbs	16 Home Life 17 Hum. Anecd. 9 Cur. Events 30 School 1 Vocations 8 Fam. People 11 Fairy Tales	30 School 8 Fam. People 9 Cur. Events 18 Ind. Titles 27 Proverbs 1 Vocations 23 Music	12 Getting Rich 1 Vocations 16 Home Life 23 Music	19 Leisure Act. 12 Getting Rich 15 Hist. Events 27 Proverbs 8 Fam. People 11 Fairy Tales 1 Vocations 23 Music 25 People 9 Cur. Events 4 Art	11 Fairy Tales 16 Home Life 10 Ethics 2 Adventure 30 School 23 Music 20 Literature 12 Getting Rich 34 Sympathy 3 Animals 27 Proverbs 36 Win. Prizes 1 Vocations 15 Hist. Events 25 People 8 Fam. People 9 Cur. Events 19 Leisure Act. 4 Art 33 Soc. Prob. 22 Mod. Ind. 7 Civics
Boys and Girls	30 School	1 Vocations 15 Hist. Events 30 School	30 School	1 Vocations 12 Getting Rich 8 Fam. People 9 Cur. Events	19 Leisure Act. 18 Ind. Titles 1 Vocations 12 Getting Rich 8 Fam. People 9 Cur. Events 23 Music 25 People 15 Hist. Events 22 Mod. Ind.	16 Home Life 19 Leisure Act. 28 Pup. Employment 12 Getting Rich 8 Fam. People 25 People 3 Animals 22 Mod. Ind. 15 Hist. Events

within these limits. Table XXX gives those categories of interest which were discarded.

ANALYSIS OF THE RANK ORDER LISTS [3]

What topics are commonly liked and disliked throughout secondary school grades by both boys and girls? By boys? By girls? Are there any sex differences? Are there topics which become more or less interesting as pupils advance through school? It is the purpose of this analysis to give such answers to these questions as may be found in the data.

Likes and Dislikes Common to All Grades

The following lists contain those topics commonly liked and those commonly disliked by boys and girls in all secondary school grades. The topics are arranged on the basis of the average position held on each of the six separate lists; for example, Travel heads the list of likes, since it ranked first in each grade list (see Table XXXVI) and the average of these six rankings is one (1).

TABLE XXXI

COMPOSITION TOPIC LIKES AND DISLIKES COMMON TO ALL GRADES FOR BOYS AND GIRLS TOGETHER

LIKED	DISLIKED
Travel	Sentiment
Adventure	Children
Outdoor Activities	Health
Ethics	Handwork
Athletics and Sports	Social Problems
Personal Experience	Science
Literature	Fairy Tales
Humorous Anecdotes	Civics
Sympathy	Proverbs
Animals*	Art
Home Life*	Winning Prizes***
Pupil Employment*	Machines****
Leisure Activities**	

[3] In this discussion each interest is designated by a shortened title. The abbreviations are used solely for economy of space.

* These three topics were dropped from the twelfth grade list because they had no more than chance ratings. They are retained on this list because of the pronounced trend through the other five grades.

** Leisure Activities stands high on all lists through the tenth grade without any indication of becoming disliked. It was removed from the eleventh and twelfth grade lists because of the chance

Table XXXI leaves eleven topics unaccounted for. The following chart gives the data concerning them; topics were dropped from the list wherever the chance character of the data warranted it.

Topic	Liked in Grades	Dropped in Grades	Disliked in Grades
Vocations	12	8, 10, 11	7, 9
Current Events	7, 8, 9, 12	10, 11	
Famous People	7, 8, 9	10, 11, 12	
Getting Rich	7, 8, 9	10, 11, 12	
Historic Events		8, 11, 12	7, 9, 10
Indefinite Titles	8, 10, 12	11	7, 9
Modern Industries		11, 12	7, 8, 9, 10
Music	12	11	7, 8, 9, 10
People		11, 12	7, 8, 9, 10
Religion	7, 8 (slightly)		9, 10, 11, 12
School	10, 11, 12	7, 8, 9	

It is evident that no definite conclusion can be made concerning Vocations. Apparently, if a complete set of likes and dislikes were made for the typical junior high school grades, the following would have to be added to Table XXXI:

Liked	Disliked
Current Events	Modern Industries
Famous People	Music
Getting Rich	People

It is indicated that Historic Events and Religion become increasingly disliked as pupils move through school; similarly, Indefinite Titles and School tend to become popular.

---

nature of its data. The pronounced liking for it in the first four grades, together with the trend in the twelfth, suggests that a larger population in these last two grades would not reverse the trend.

  *** Winning Prizes is included on this list because of pronounced trend for being disliked. In the twelfth grade it has a neutral median.

  **** Machines is retained on the list of dislikes, even though it is liked by both boys and girls in the twelfth grade. Twelfth grade girls rank it third among the most disliked topics. The topic is popular with boys and it is undoubtedly true that the boys' liking greatly affected the twelfth grade median, since the boys constitute 57 per cent of the twelfth grade pupils.

TABLE XXXII
Composition Topic Likes and Dislikes Common to Boys in All Grades

Likes	Dislikes
Travel	Sentiment
Outdoor Activities	Children
Athletics and Sports	Fairy Tales
Adventure	Handwork
Current Events*	Health
Ethics	Social Problems
Machines*	Proverbs
Famous People*	Art
Leisure Activities*	Civics
Pupil Employment	Religion
	Science*
	Winning Prizes*

*These titles are placed on these lists subject to the following conditions, which do not seem to change the trends:

Current Events	Dropped in Grade 11
Machines	Dropped in Grade 8
Famous People	Dropped in Grade 12
Leisure Activities	Dropped in Grades 11 and 12
Science	Dropped in Grade 11
Winning Prizes	Median 3.000 in Grade 12

The lists above omit fourteen topics. The following chart gives the data concerning them.

Topics	Liked in Grades	Dropped in Grades	Disliked in Grades
Vocations	10, 11, 12	8, 9	7
Animals	7, 8, 9, 10	11, 12	
Getting Rich	7, 8, 11	9, 10, 12	
Historic Events		7, 8, 9, 10, 11, 12	
Home Life	12 slightly	11, 12	7, 8, 9
Humorous Anecdotes		7, 9, 11, 12	8, 10
Indefinite Titles		10, 11, 12	7, 8, 9
Literature	7, 8, 9, 10, 11	12	
Modern Industries	8, 10	7, 9, 11, 12	
Music		11, 12	7, 8, 9, 10
People		11, 12	7, 8, 9, 10
Personal Experience	8, 12	9, 11	7, 10
School	11	9, 10, 12	7, 8
Sympathy	7, 9, 10, 11		8, 12

Here again, a division for junior high school pupils is warranted. The preferences and dislikes of junior high school boys require the following additions to the list of topics common to boys in all grades:

Likes	Dislikes
Animals	Home Life
Getting Rich	Indefinite Titles
Literature	Music
	People
	School

Historic Events is dropped from consideration in all grades. It is probable that Personal Experience is liked more by boys in the later grades. Boys appear to be indifferent, tending toward dislike, about Humorous Anecdotes, Modern Industries, and Sympathy (the last two have medians close to 3.000).

TABLE XXXIII

Composition Topic Likes and Dislikes Common to Girls in All Grades

Likes	Dislikes
Travel	Machines
Adventure*	Science
Personal Experience	Health
Outdoor Activities	Handwork
Ethics*	Civics*
Literature*	Sentiment
Animals*	Social Problems
Humorous Anecdotes*	People*
Sympathy*	Children
	Art*
	Historic Events*
	Modern Industries*
	Winning Prizes*

* These titles are retained on these lists subject to the following conditions, which do not appear to change the trends:

Adventure, Ethics, Literature, Animals, Sympathy, Civics, Social Problems	Dropped in Grade 12
Art, Historic Events, Modern Industries, People	Dropped in Grades 11 and 12
Humorous Anecdotes	Dropped in Grade 8

Winning Prizes is liked a little in the seventh grade and disliked in all but the twelfth grade, where it is dropped.

The lists above omit fourteen topics. The following chart gives the data concerning them.

54 *Written Composition Interests of High School Pupils*

Topic	Liked in Grades	Dropped in Grades	Disliked in Grades
Vocations............		8, 9, 10, 11, 12	7
Athletics and Sports....	8, 9, 10, 11, 12		7
Famous People.......		7, 8, 9, 11, 12	10
Current Events.......		8, 9, 11, 12	7, 10
Fairy Tales...........		7, 8, 11, 12	9, 10
Getting Rich.........	7, 8, 9	10, 11, 12	
Home Life...........	9, 11	7, 8, 10, 12	
Indefinite Titles.......	10, 11, 12	9	7, 8
Leisure Activities......	7, 8, 9, 10	11, 12	
Music................		9, 10, 11, 12	7, 8
Proverbs.............	10	7, 9, 11, 12	8
Pupil Employment....	7, 8, 9, 10, 11	12	
Religion.............	7, 8, 9		10, 11, 12
School...............	10, 11	7, 8, 9, 12	

Vocations, Famous People, Current Events, Fairy Tales, Home Life, and Proverbs are dropped in so many grades that definite conclusions concerning them cannot be made.

Additions to the junior high school list of girls' interests are as follows:

Liked	Disliked
Getting Rich	Indefinite Titles
Leisure Activities	Music
Pupil Employment	
Religion	

Among senior high school girls, the following topics develop pronounced preferences: Athletics and Sports, Indefinite Titles, and School.

Effect on the Combined Lists of Pronounced Preference or Dislike by Boys or Girls

If the separate lists of preferences for boys and girls are compared with the preferences for boys and girls combined, it can be seen which titles were placed on the combined list by the predominant preference of one sex. Such a comparison would give the following lists: Topics placed on the combined list by the pronounced preference of

Boys: Athletics and Sports, Leisure Activities, Pupil Employment.
Girls: Home Life, Humorous Anecdotes, Personal Experience, Sympathy.

A similar comparison for dislikes provides the following lists: Topics placed on the combined list of dislikes by the pronounced dislike of

Boys: Proverbs.
Girls: Machines and Modern Industries.

Sex Differences in Choices of Composition Topics

The influence of sex differences appears in the selection of those topics in which there is a real difference between the choices of the boys and those of the girls. To locate these differences, the separate lists for each sex in each grade were compared. The per cents of B and NB choices were totaled for each topic (except those disregarded because of the chance character of their data). Then the standard error of this total for each topic was computed by the formula referred to previously: $\sigma_p = \sqrt{\frac{pq}{N}}$. The standard error of the difference between the two per cents was obtained by use of the formula for the standard error of the difference between two independent variables: $\sigma_d = \sqrt{\sigma_1^2 + \sigma_2^2}$.[4] Whenever the difference between the per cents was greater than three times the standard error of the difference, that difference was considered real. The resulting lists, given in Table XXXIV, contain these items, without reference to the relative preference or dislike for the topic; for instance, in the seventh, eighth, and ninth grades Sentiment appears on the girls' list, even though it is ranked near the bottom of the rank order lists by each sex. Nevertheless, the difference in choice is a real one, the interpretation being that more girls than boys in these grades would be likely to choose that topic for a composition.

Table XXXIV reveals that practically throughout the secondary school grades, some topics are preferred more by one sex than by the other. These sex differences are given in Table XXXV according to the sex preferring the topic.

In the junior high school grades Handwork and Outdoor Activities are preferred more by the boys, while girls like the topics: Children, Religion, and Sentiment. In the senior high school grades boys prefer Vocations and Pupil Employment.

[4] Kelley, Truman L., op. cit., p. 182.

TABLE XXXIV

GRADE LISTS OF COMPOSITION TOPIC INTERESTS ARRANGED BY SEXES

Boys

Grade 7	Grade 8	Grade 9	Grade 10	Grade 11	Grade 12
Athletics	Athletics	Athletics	Athletics	Vocations Athletics	Vocations Athletics
Current Events Famous People Handwork Machines Mod. Industries Outdoor Act.	Current Events Famous People Handwork Machines Outdoor Act.	Current Events Famous People Machines Mod. Industries Outdoor Act. Pupil Emp.	Current Events Famous People Handwork Machines Mod. Industries Pupil Emp.	Current Events Famous People Machines Mod. Industries Science	Current Events Machines Mod. Industries Pupil Emp. Leisure Act.

Girls

Grade 7	Grade 8	Grade 9	Grade 10	Grade 11	Grade 12
Children Home Life Personal Exp. Proverbs Religion Sentiment Sympathy Travel	Children Home Life Personal Exp. Religion Sentiment Travel Getting Rich Hum. Anecdotes Indef. Titles School	Children Home Life Personal Exp. Religion Sentiment Sympathy Travel School Literature	Children Home Life Personal Exp. Proverbs Religion Sympathy Travel Hum. Anecdotes Indef. Titles School Art	Home Life Personal Exp. Proverbs Sympathy Travel Hum. Anecdotes Indef. Titles	Home Life

TABLE XXXV

SEX PREFERENCES IN COMPOSITION TOPIC INTERESTS COMMON TO ALL GRADES

Boys	Girls
Athletics Current Events Famous People Machines Modern Industries	Home Life Personal Experience Sympathy Travel

TABLE XXXVI

Composition Topic Likes and Dislikes Common to Both Boys and Girls, with Medians

Likes

Grade 7		Grade 8		Grade 9		Grade 10		Grade 11		Grade 12	
Travel	3.080	Travel	3.102	Travel	3.086	Travel	3.072	Travel	3.096	Travel	3.098
Adventure	3.065	Adventure	3.069	Adventure	3.059	Adventure	3.049	Athletics	3.064	Athletics	3.063
Out. Act.	3.054	Out. Act.	3.053	Out. Act.	3.053	Out. Act.	3.046	Out. Act.	3.048	Out. Act.	3.043
Animals	3.053	Ethics	3.041	Ethics	3.039	Athletics	3.042	Adventure	3.038	Per. Exp.	3.040
Get. Rich	3.046	Animals	3.040	Lei. Act.	3.033	Ethics	3.037	Ethics	3.031		
Lei. Act.	3.036	Get. Rich	3.030	Athletics	3.029	Lei. Act.	3.037	Lit.	3.027		
Literature	3.035	Lei. Act.	3.030	Animals	3.028	Lit.	3.026	School	3.026		
Ethics	3.028	Lit.	3.029	Lit.	3.024	Animals	3.011	Sympathy	3.014		
Pup. Emp.	3.014	Athletics	3.023	Pup. Emp.	3.014	Sympathy	3.010	Pup. Emp.	3.007		
Sympathy	3.009	Per. Exp.	3.018	Sympathy	3.011	Pup. Emp.	3.009				
		Pup. Emp.	3.012								

Dislikes

Grade 7		Grade 8		Grade 9		Grade 10		Grade 11		Grade 12	
Sentiment	2.935	Sentiment	2.942	Sentiment	2.941	Sentiment	2.940	Sentiment	2.927	Children	2.917
Health	2.954	Children	2.952	Children	2.946	Children	2.952	Handwork	2.942	Handwork	2.925
Children	2.963	Soc. Prob.	2.956	Fairy Tales	2.962	Fairy Tales	2.957	Children	2.942	Sentiment	2.927
People	2.965	Health	2.958	Science	2.964	Health	2.958	Health	2.945	Health	2.934
Science	2.968	Proverbs	2.965	Handwork	2.964	Handwork	2.960	Civics	2.958	Religion	2.955
Soc. Prob.	2.968	People	2.968	Soc. Prob.	2.971	Civics	2.968	Soc. Prob.	2.966	Science	2.965
Music	2.969	Ind. Title	2.968	Civics	2.972	Science	2.972	Religion	2.974		
Ind. Titles	2.970	Science	2.970	People	2.976	Soc. Prob.	2.982	Win Prizes	2.991		
Civics	2.973	Music	2.971	Health	2.979	Religion	2.987				
Handwork	2.977	Handwork	2.974	Art	2.984	Art	2.991				
Art	2.989	Civics	2.978	Win Prizes	2.996	Win Prizes	2.994				
School	2.993	Art	2.983			People	2.998				
Vocations	2.996	Win Prizes	2.994								

Changes in Interest Between the Seventh and Twelfth Grades

A comparison of the lists of interests for the seventh and the twelfth grade would show which topics, if any, are subject to a change in interest as pupils pass through school. For this comparison the technique of the standard error of the difference between two independent variables was again employed. The resulting lists indicate the topics in which the difference in preference is real, the topics being listed under the grade which has the greatest preference.

	SEVENTH GRADE	TWELFTH GRADE
Boys and Girls	Adventure Animals Children Current Events Getting Rich Literature Religion	Vocations Athletics Machines Music People
Boys	Animals Famous People Current Events Getting Rich Literature Religion	Vocations Athletics Humorous Anecdotes Machines Music Personal Experience
Girls	Adventure Animals Children Getting Rich Leisure Activities Pupil Employment Religion	Athletics Fairy Tales Machines Music

A Comparison of the Findings of This Investigation with the Reading Interests Reported by Jordan and Washburne

Jordan's list distinguishes between the interests of boys and of girls. Washburne's does not. The ages and the grades reported do not coincide with any but the seventh and eighth grades of the composition investigation. By grouping topics on the Jordan and the Washburne lists, a comparison can be made. Following are the groupings used:

Adventure
    War and scouting   Indians and cowboys
    Strenuous adventure   War heroes
    On having things happen   Danger
    Mysteries   Pirates
    Having new experiences of almost any kind
Animals
    Dogs and animals
Athletics and Sports
    School and sports
    Physical strength and aptitude
Children
    Children
Ethics
    Being loyal   Good moral character

Composition Interests Shown by Pupils' Choices

    In unselfishness   In being honest at school
    Self-sacrifice
    Self-control, particularly in critical situations
    Being honest, straightforward, open, trustworthy
    In being honorable and possessing a clean mind
Fairy Tales
    Fairyland
Getting Rich
    Getting rich
Handwork
    What-and-how-to-do books
Home Life
    In being useful at home
Humorous Anecdotes
    In playing pranks at school
Sentiment
    In being loved and admired for oneself
    Love or romance
Sympathy
    Kindness to others, especially those who are in distress
    Calling forth sympathy
Travel
    Going somewhere
    In going to a city, if brought up in the country
    Travel

This list includes thirteen items. The classifications are arbitrary, but they have been made with a view to combining those items which have a common meaning. School is omitted because it occurs on the reading lists combined with other items and therefore appears on the lists in other classifications.

Comparison of the two different sets of interests discloses the following interests of boys and girls common to reading and composition:

    Adventure
    Animals
    Ethics
    Getting Rich
    Travel

The following reading interests are not liked as composition topics:

    Children
    Sentiment
    Fairy Tales [5]

Boys like to write as well as to read about Athletics and Sports; their liking for Handwork is confined to a reading interest.

[5] The evidence for girls is not conclusive, but indicative.

Girls like to write as well as to read about Humorous Anecdotes and Sympathy; there is inconclusive evidence about their liking to write on Home Life.

Conclusions

1. Of the thirty-six categories of interest used in this investigation, the following topics [6] are commonly liked and disliked, respectively, by boys and girls in all secondary school grades:

Liked	Disliked
Travel	Sentiment
Adventure	Children
Outdoor Activities	Health
Ethics	Handwork
Athletics and Sports	Social Problems
Personal Experience	Science
Literature	Fairy Tales
Humorous Anecdotes	Civics
Sympathy	Proverbs
Animals	Art
Home Life	Winning Prizes
Pupil Employment	Machines
Leisure Activities	

The following are additional junior high school likes and dislikes common to all pupils:

Current Events	Modern Industries
Famous People	Music
Getting Rich	People

2. The following lists contain topics for which one sex or the other has a preference or dislike pronounced enough to place these topics on the list of likes or dislikes common to all grades.

Boys

Liked	Disliked
Athletics and Sports	Proverbs
Leisure Activities	
Pupil Employment	

Girls

Home Life	Machines
Humorous Anecdotes	Modern Industries
Personal Experience	
Sympathy	

[6] Refer to Table I for complete definitions of the shortened topic headings used throughout these conclusions.

3. In addition to the likes and dislikes common to both boys and girls in all grades, there are topics which are commonly liked, or disliked, by boys alone, as follows:

Liked	Disliked
Current Events	Religion
Machines	
Famous People	

Boys in the junior high school grades like, or dislike, the following:

Animals	Home Life
Literature	Indefinite Titles
	School

4. There are no topics liked solely by girls throughout all grades which are not liked by boys. Dislikes common to girls only follow:

Liked	Disliked
None	Historic Events

Girls in the junior high school grades like, or dislike, the following:

Leisure Activities	Indefinite Titles
Pupil Employment	
Religion	

5. The topics more likely to be preferred in all grades by one sex than by the other are as follows:

By boys: Athletics, Current Events, Famous People, Machines, Modern Industries.
  In junior high school grades: Handwork and Outdoor Activities.
  In senior high school grades: Vocations and Pupil Employment.

By girls: Home Life, Personal Experience, Sympathy, Travel.
  In junior high school grades: Children, Religion, Sentiment.
  In senior high school grades: None.

6. It is evident that interests in topics for written compositions vary from grade to grade. The differences, as indicated by topics more preferred by boys and girls together in the seventh grade than in the twelfth grade, and vice versa, are as follows:

Seventh Grade: Adventure, Animals, Children, Current Events, Getting Rich, Literature, Religion.
Twelfth Grade: Vocations, Athletics, Machines, Music, People.

7. There is a variety of composition topic interests among secondary school pupils. This is true of both sexes, combined or considered separately. No topic is entirely liked or disliked in any of the groups. There are evidences always of differences among pupils of the same group. It is therefore evident that if interest is a factor to be considered in making assignments for written composition, considerable latitude in the choice of topics should be permitted.

8. Reading and composition-writing interests which coincide (in the seventh and eighth grades) are as follows:

Boys and Girls: Adventure, Animals, Ethics, Getting Rich, Travel.
Boys: Athletics and Sports.
Girls: Humorous Anecdotes and Sympathy.

Reading interests which are not liked as composition topics are as follows:

Boys and Girls: Children, Sentiment, Fairy Tales.
Boys: Handwork.
Girls: None.

CHAPTER V

PUPILS' REASONS FOR CHOOSING SPECIFIC TITLES

Why pupils make the choices they do is very properly a part of the problem of pupils' written composition interests. Adequate knowledge of this phase of the problem would be an important factor in the control and guidance of interests. While it is undoubtedly true that pupils do not write from any one simple motive, if we can find out why pupils think they make their choices, the information may serve to orient the chief problems, even if it does not contribute a direct answer. For this reason, pupils were asked to write on the backs of their slips an answer to the following question: Why did you choose the topic you did?

The A list of composition titles was composed of the titles having the highest rankings given by the expert rankers. If there is any choice, this list contained the best titles submitted. A classification of the replies given on this list would include practically every pupil who took part in the entire study and would probably provide 3,500 replies which should give reliable information, as compared to what might be obtained by classifying all the answers. Thus, the results given in this study are separate lists for boys and girls, respectively, by grades taken from the replies given on the A list.

To arrive at a basis for grouping the replies, about one hundred were sorted and the broad groups were defined. With some modifications, sixteen classes of reasons were made. An effort was made to define distinct reasons, as pupils gave them, for writing compositions. Some few teachers failed to have their pupils write the reasons. Some few pupils failed to state a reason. Some replies were illegible and had to be discarded. Occasionally pupils gave irrelevant reasons for writing a composition on a specific topic; for example, when a pupil chose title 29—Why I Go to Sunday School—instead of telling why he chose the title he told why he went to Sunday School. In one such case the pupil said he went to Sunday School to learn about God. It seemed (1) rather obvious that the pupil had misunderstood the directions, and (2) that it would not be fair to say that the child had written the composition to learn about God, that is, that his reason for liking the title could not be construed as a reason for writing about the title. Such reasons were also discarded. If it were assumed in such cases that the pupil wrote on the title because he liked the subject, the results would not be altered materially. In the seventh grade, eleven girls and twenty-two boys gave irrelevant reasons, but more than 40 per cent of the classified replies (from more than eight hundred) have already been included in this category.

The following sixteen categories of reasons were eventually defined. The headings used should be looked upon as abbreviations for the full definitions given here.

1. ADVENTURE

    This classification was used when a pupil said specifically that he chose a title because an exciting or thrilling story or composition could be written about it. The story or account itself would be thrilling, as distinguished from the thrill to be obtained from the act of writing, which falls under group six.

2. BEST COMPOSITION

    Some pupils said frankly that they chose a particular title because they felt they could write their best composition or theme on that subject.

    Others implied this idea when they said "this was the best title," "this was a good title," or "this title appealed to me." They did not say they were interested in that which the title represented. Our inference was that the wording or implications of the title had an appeal which made a pupil feel he could write acceptably on that topic.

3. CHARACTER

    Qualities of high moral character were used by some pupils as reasons for choosing one topic above all others for written compositions. In this classification are those reasons in which pupils said they "admired" some person, that they wrote about a person because he or she was a hero or heroine, or because some person possessed a certain quality, such as bravery, compassion, or the like.

    Occasionally some pupils wrote about abstract qualities of character, extolling them as qualities for a chum or as "good" for anyone to have.

4. CURRENT INTEREST

    This class is distinguished from the one in which pupils knew about a particular thing or had experienced it (group 10), as past is distinguished from present. Some pupils gave a present interest in a topic as a reason for writing about it. The word "just" often served to distinguish it; the pupil specified that just now this particular thing interested him and, from the way his reason was worded, it would seem safe to add, it probably interested him more than anything else. From the standpoint of interests, it held the stage at the time of writing the composition and, in that sense, was temporary. Recency of contact served as a criterion. When a pupil specified that a certain thing was his hobby, it was included in this group.

5. EASIEST

In this classification the pupil has said or clearly indicated that this topic was the easiest to write about. Most often the word "easy" appeared in the reason given. Just what the pupil meant may be a matter for speculation. It is probably true that a majority had in mind expending a minimum of effort on an assignment which held no special significance for them. Others may have felt that the writing and organizing would be easy; that is to say, they felt that the best composition could be produced on this topic, because they possessed more information about it than about any other, or were more familiar with it. Whatever the cause, the classification was made because the pupil recognized in one topic the least difficult or laborious of several tasks.

6. ENJOY WRITING

The key to this class is that the pupil says he enjoys or is interested in writing about the topic he has chosen. He uses the word "write" and emphasizes the point that writing about this topic is enjoyable or interesting.

7. ETHICAL

In this group are included those reasons pupils gave in which an ethical motive was dominant. Pupils said they chose a particular topic because "we ought or we ought not to do" so-and-so, or we ought to know. Others expressed this motive by saying this would be a "good thing," especially "if we all did it." Others said some particular thing was an important thing in life.

The reason was interpreted to mean that the pupil wrote on his topic because he was concerned about the way people ought to act. It is differentiated from group 13 because the predominant idea was the discussion of the behavior problem rather than a desire to expound a personal opinion.

8. EXPECTATION

A motive for writing about a particular topic was expressed by some pupils as a wish to have, to do, or to be some particular thing. Others spoke of it as an ambition; still others wrote on a topic because they were planning something or would like to "plan" something. The ideas of wishing for and being ambitious about some one thing were grouped under what may be termed unattained desires. In each case the desire was given as the chief motive for writing.

9. HUMOR

In this group are included those replies which implied that a pupil chose a specific topic because the product would be a humorous or funny story or composition.

10. KNOWLEDGE

Some pupils wrote on a particular topic because, they said, they had more than common information or knowledge of a topic—they had visited a factory, had been in a certain place, had bought a gift, had made camp, or had been through an unforgettable experience. They wrote from a background of experience, through having done a particular thing or having been party to a particular event.

11. My Opinion

This group seemed necessary because so many pupils used phrases similar to these: I wanted to tell, or I think so-and-so. Included here were all reasons in which a pupil seemed called upon to impress one with the idea that he was compelled by some inner force to tell his opinion. Those were included which said, "This gives me a chance to tell what I, etc."

12. Reading

In this group are those reasons in which a pupil said he wrote about a particular topic solely or chiefly because he had read much about it—not because he liked reading.

13. Topic

This class distinguishes between liking to write about and liking a topic. In effect, the pupil says simply, "I chose this topic because I am interested in machines"—or whatever it may be. He does not say he likes to write about machines. The distinction is made because the pupil says he is much interested in a topic but not necessarily moved to write about it. We do not know what mental reservations he makes, but it is likely that the writing is a very secondary consideration and a particular topic, with or without step-by-step reasoning, is used, as if the pupil said to himself, "I like this thing; since I must write a composition, I cannot do better than to use this as something to write about."

14. Sole Choice

In this category of reasons were included all those in which pupils specifically said (1) they did not like any others but the one chosen, or (2) the one they chose was the only one on the list about which they could write.

15. Universal Interest

A few pupils gave as their reason for writing on a subject the fact that practically everyone was interested in it or knew about it. Universality of interest was given or implied as the reason for writing upon a given topic.

16. Unclassified

In this group are included all those reasons which were not classified under any heading and which occurred in such small numbers that our purpose would be better served by listing these reasons separately.

These definitions of reasons were used to classify 3,411 replies from boys and girls in the six secondary school grades. The total replies by sex and grade were as follows:

Grade	Boys	Girls
7	363	386
8	367	397
9	439	467
10	346	304
11	112	186
12	28	16
Total	1,655	1,756

The data for the eleventh and twelfth grades are too few to be conclusive. Nevertheless, they do not seem to reverse the trends of the other grades.

TABLE XXXVII
RANK ORDER LISTS OF PUPILS' REASONS FOR CHOOSING SPECIFIC TOPICS

Boys

Grade 7	Grade 8	Grade 9	Grade 10	Grade 11	Grade 12
Knowledge	Ethical	Knowledge	Knowledge	Knowledge	Expectation
Expectation	Knowledge	Enjoy Writing	Best Comp.	Unclassified	Knowledge
Enjoy Writing	Expectation	Expectation	Enjoy Writing	Cur. Interest	Best Comp.
Best Comp.	Enjoy Writing	Best Comp.	Unclassified	Expectation	My Opinion
Character	Best Comp.	Unclassified	Character	Enjoy Writing	Unclassified
Unclassified *	Adventure	Character	Expectation	Best Comp.	Cur. Interest
Adventure	Cur. Interest	Easiest	Adventure	Easiest	Enjoy Writing
My Opinion	Character	Ethical	Cur. Interest	Sole Choice	Sole Choice
Cur. Interest	My Opinion	My Opinion	Easiest	Character	Univ. Interest
Ethical	Reading	Cur. Interest	Ethical	Ethical	Adventure
Sole Choice	Easiest	Sole Choice	My Opinion	My Opinion	Character
Easiest	Unclassified	Adventure	Sole Choice	Reading	Easiest
Humor	Sole Choice	Reading	Reading	Univ. Interest	Ethical
Reading	Humor	Humor	Univ. Interest	Humor	Humor
Univ. Interest	Univ. Interest	Univ. Interest	Humor	Adventure	Reading

Girls

Grade 7	Grade 8	Grade 9	Grade 10	Grade 11	Grade 12
Knowledge	Knowledge	Knowledge	Knowledge	Knowledge	Best Comp.
Enjoy Writing	Enjoy Writing	Enjoy Writing	Enjoy Writing	Unclassified	Knowledge
Expectation	Expectation	Best Comp.	Best Comp.	Enjoy Writing	Character
Best Comp.	Best Comp.	Expectation	Unclassified	Expectation	Cur. Interest
Sole Choice	Ethical	Easiest	Expectation	My Opinion	Unclassified
Ethical	Unclassified	Unclassified	My Opinion	Best Comp.	Adventure
My Opinion	Adventure	Adventure	Cur. Interest	Ethical	Easiest
Adventure	My Opinion	Character	Easiest	Cur. Interest	Enjoy Writing
Character	Character	Cur. Interest	Ethical	Sole Choice	Ethical
Cur. Interest	Cur. Interest	My Opinion	Sole Choice	Univ. Interest	Expectation
Unclassified	Easiest	Ethical	Character	Character	Humor
Easiest	Reading	Reading	Reading	Easiest	My Opinion
Humor	Sole Choice	Sole Choice	Adventure	Reading	Reading
Reading	Univ. Interest	Univ. Interest	Univ. Interest	Adventure	Sole Choice
Univ. Interest	Humor	Humor	Humor	Humor	Univ. Interest

* Unclassified reasons are listed in Appendix V.

Table XXXVII gives rank order lists of the reasons pupils give for choosing specific topics for composition. The lists are arranged for each sex by grades. Table XXXVIII gives the per cent of boys and of girls in each grade selecting each reason.

68   Written Composition Interests of High School Pupils

TABLE XXXVIII
Rank Order Lists of Per Cents of Pupils Giving Particular Reasons for Choosing Specific Topics *

Boys

Grade 7 N-363		Grade 8 N-367		Grade 9 N-439		Grade 10 N-346		Grade 11 N-112		Grade 12 N-28	
I	II	I	II	I	II	I	II	I	II	I	II
13	43	13	35	13	43	13	41	13	31	13	29
10	20	7	14	10	13	10	15	10	24	8	18
8	6	10	14	6	8	2	7	16	11	10	14
6	4	8	9	8	8	6	7	4	7	2	11
2	4	6	8	2	7	16	5	8	5	11	6
3	4	2	5	16	5	3	4	6	4	16	6
16	4	1	4	3	4	8	4	2	3	4	4
1	3	4	4	5	3	1	3	5	3	6	4
11	3	3	3	7	3	4	3	14	3	14	4
4	2	11	2	11	3	5	3	3	2	15	4
7	2	12	2	4	2	7	3	7	2	1	0
14	2	5	1	14	2	11	3	11	2	3	0
5	1	16	1	1	1	14	3	12	2	5	0
9	1	14	1	12	1	12	1	15	2	7	0
12	1	9	1	9	1	15	1	9	1	9	0
15	1	15	1	15	1	9	0	1	0	12	0
	101		105		105		103		100		100

Girls

Grade 7 N-386		Grade 8 N-397		Grade 9 N-467		Grade 10 N-304		Grade 11 N-186		Grade 12 N-16	
I	II	I	II	I	II	I	II	I	II	I	II
13	42	13	37	13	37	13	26	13	26	13	50
10	16	10	15	10	18	10	24	10	18	2	19
6	10	6	11	6	9	6	9	14	14	10	12
8	8	8	9	2	8	2	7	6	11	3	6
2	6	2	7	8	7	16	7	8	7	4	6
14	4	7	4	5	4	8	5	11	7	16	6
7	3	16	4	16	4	11	4	2	4	1	0
11	3	1	3	1	2	4	3	7	4	5	0
1	2	11	3	3	2	5	3	4	3	6	0
3	2	3	2	4	2	7	3	14	3	7	0
4	2	4	1	11	2	14	3	15	2	8	0
16	2	5	1	7	1	3	2	3	1	9	0
5	1	12	1	12	1	12	2	5	1	11	0
9	1	14	1	14	1	1	1	12	1	12	0
12	0	15	1	15	1	15	1	1	0	14	0
15	0	9	0	9	0	9	0	9	0	15	0
	102		100		99		100		102		99

* Column I gives the number assigned to each specific reason; column II gives the per cent of pupils selecting each reason.

Analysis of the Data

The chief reason for writing a composition, given in every grade, is that the pupil likes the topic he wrote about. The second most common reason is that the pupil has some knowledge of the topic he chose or some information about it. These two reasons account for at least one-half of all the replies, except in grades eleven and twelve, where all replies are included within 40 per cent.

The next three most common reasons for writing compositions are: (1) the pupil expects to see or do the thing he writes about; (2) he likes to write about the topic he chose; and (3) he thought he could write the best composition on the topic he chose.

These five reasons account for at least two-thirds of all the reasons given in each grade by each sex.

Conclusions

1. The five chief reasons pupils give for choosing their titles for compositions are as follows:

    They like the topic they chose.
    They have some special knowledge about the topic.
    They like to write about the topic of their choice.
    They expect to see or do the topic they wrote about.
    They think they can write the best composition about this topic.

2. Liking a topic and having especial information about it are the two reasons most frequently given by children for choosing specific topics for written composition.

3. There are no pronounced sex differences in assigning reasons for choosing topics for written compositions.

4. Pupils in secondary schools appear to have a variety of reasons for choosing particular topics for written composition.

5. There is an indication that as pupils enter the senior secondary school grades, they have more complex reasons for choosing particular titles.

CHAPTER VI

WRITTEN DISCOURSE PREFERENCES OF SECONDARY SCHOOL PUPILS

The investigation of the mediums which secondary school pupils prefer for written discourse was outlined in Chapter II. The questionnaire was handed to pupils at some time during the composition-writing investigation. Pupils merely marked the questionnaire. They were not asked to write as they were in the topic-preference investigation. Nevertheless, there is reason to believe that the data represent accurately the topics which pupils think they prefer. In the first place, ranking four items out of ten is a task short enough to prevent fatigue and loss of interest; and it is quite certain that the four items ranked will represent real choices because, usually, the pupil is asked to choose on the basis of one from two and a half. In the second place, there is evidence that the pupils went at the task earnestly; in the preliminary use of the questionnaire, the writer found most of the pupils much interested in it and quite eager to discuss their choices after their papers had been collected. Several teachers in Kalamazoo sent word that their pupils were much interested in the investigation. Though it was not sought, no word of a listless use of the questionnaire was received.

For the most part, pupils understood and followed directions perfectly. It is safe to say that not more than 3 per cent of the returned papers had to be discarded for illegibility or failure to follow directions. A total of returns for 4,660 pupils were tabulated. Table XXXIX gives by grade, sex, and city the number of pupils who participated, together with the number using each form of the questionnaire.

The data of this study were treated by methods similar to those of the topic interest study. Replies were tabulated on the following basis: a rating of B was assigned a numerical value of 5; NB, 4; no rating, 3; NL, 2; L, 1. From these tabulations, medians for each type were computed and the types were placed in rank order lists according to their medians. Medians above 3.000 were interpreted

Written Discourse Preferences of High School Pupils

TABLE XXXIX
Returns on the Types of Discourse Questionnaires *

Grade	City	Boys Forms					Girls Forms					Boys and Girls Forms				
		A	B	C	D	Total	A	B	C	D	Total	A	B	C	D	Total
7	K	79	84	60	64	287	76	66	89	88	319	155	150	149	152	606
	SF	12	11	11	5	39	8	6	7	10	31	20	17	18	15	70
	H	25	19	16	20	80	20	23	30	22	95	45	42	46	42	175
	Total	116	114	87	89	406	104	95	126	120	445	220	209	213	209	851
8	K	61	70	66	58	255	77	63	78	83	301	138	133	144	141	556
	SF	9	4	7	12	32	7	2	7	8	24	16	6	14	20	56
	H	28	19	24	28	99	18	22	23	16	79	46	41	47	44	178
	Total	98	93	97	98	386	102	87	108	107	404	200	180	205	205	790
9	K	66	75	72	58	271	68	67	72	77	284	134	142	144	135	555
	SF	7	12	9	10	38	11	6	10	8	35	18	18	19	18	73
	H	32	36	27	30	125	25	22	24	19	90	57	58	51	49	215
	Total	105	123	108	98	434	104	95	106	104	409	209	218	214	202	843
10	K	70	76	61	74	281	76	70	80	73	299	146	146	141	147	580
	SF	7	6	6	10	29	7	7	7	6	27	14	13	13	16	56
	H	15	15	16	10	56	20	17	17	22	76	35	32	33	32	132
	WP	12	6	10	12	40	14	6	12	10	42	26	12	22	22	82
	S	97	95	87	85	364	67	70	70	71	278	164	165	157	156	642
	Total	201	198	180	191	770	184	170	186	182	722	385	368	366	373	1492
11	K	7	8	11	11	37	13	11	9	12	45	20	19	20	23	82
	SF	3	5	3	2	13	5	4	5	8	22	8	9	8	10	35
	H	13	11	12	11	47	10	14	10	13	47	23	25	22	24	94
	WP	5	9	8	6	28	8	7	7	5	27	13	16	15	11	55
	S	23	20	21	22	86	25	18	23	25	91	48	38	44	47	177
	Total	51	53	55	52	211	61	54	54	63	232	112	107	109	115	443
12	K	8	9	9	8	34	6	4	4	5	19	14	13	13	13	53
	SF	4	5	8	3	20	5	6	5	6	22	9	11	13	9	42
	H	4	7	7	4	22	9	7	9	10	35	13	14	16	14	57
	WP	7	7	3	6	23	4	6	10	7	27	11	13	13	13	50
	S	6	5	7	5	23	6	5	2	3	16	12	10	9	8	39
	Total	29	33	34	26	122	30	28	30	31	119	59	61	64	57	241
Grand Totals		600	614	561	554	2329	585	529	610	607	2331	1185	1143	1171	1161	4660

* Designations for cities are as follows: K—Kalamazoo. SF—Seneca Falls. H—Huntington. WP—White Plains. S—Stamford.

as showing a preference, and those below 3.000 as showing a dislike, since a value of 3.000 assigned to no choice was understood to be the mid-point of the interval in which the data were assumed to be distributed evenly.

Tables XL to XLV give the rank order lists for each grade for three groups: boys and girls, boys, and girls. Besides the medians, the tables include the per cent of responses for each of the five ratings for each type of discourse.

TABLE XL

RANK ORDER LIST OF WRITTEN DISCOURSE PREFERENCES BY SEVENTH GRADE

Rank	Title No.	Title	Median	Per Cent of Choices per Weight				
				5	4	3	2	1
		Boys and Girls						
1	5	Friendly Letter........	3.254	20.4	17.0	50.8	5.9	5.9
2	1	Narration.............	3.156	18.6	13.5	52.1	8.0	7.9
3	2	Description...........	3.116	12.6	12.5	65.1	6.0	3.9
4	4	Argument.............	3.113	13.4	13.2	60.5	6.3	6.6
5	8	News Article..........	2.978	4.3	7.4	73.2	10.2	4.8
6	3	Exposition............	2.960	7.1	7.9	65.0	10.1	10.0
7	9	Editorial Essay........	2.912	4.3	7.8	64.5	12.2	11.2
8	6	Business Letter........	2.878	5.9	5.5	62.0	12.1	14.5
9	7	Poetry................	2.855	8.0	9.6	50.2	13.4	18.8
10	10	Debate Brief..........	2.812	5.4	5.5	56.6	15.8	16.6
		Boys						
1	4	Argument.............	3.170	16.0	15.5	55.9	5.4	7.1
2	2	Description...........	3.130	13.5	12.3	65.2	5.2	3.7
3	5	Friendly Letter........	3.110	13.8	14.0	56.9	7.6	7.6
4	1	Narration.............	3.105	17.0	11.3	54.9	8.9	7.9
5	3	Exposition............	3.046	10.1	11.6	62.3	8.4	7.6
6	8	News Article..........	2.993	5.2	8.6	71.4	9.6	5.2
7	9	Editorial Essay........	2.928	5.9	7.1	64.6	14.0	8.4
8	6	Business Letter........	2.897	5.7	6.2	63.3	11.1	13.8
9	10	Debate Brief..........	2.861	7.4	5.9	57.4	14.3	15.0
10	7	Poetry................	2.726	5.4	7.4	48.0	15.5	23.6
		Girls						
1	5	Friendly Letter........	3.418	26.5	19.8	45.2	4.3	4.3
2	1	Narration.............	3.207	20.0	15.5	49.4	7.2	7.9
3	2	Description...........	3.104	11.7	12.6	65.0	6.7	4.0
4	4	Argument.............	3.068	11.0	11.0	64.7	7.2	6.1
5.5	7	Poetry................	2.964	10.3	11.7	52.2	11.5	14.4
5.5	8	News Article..........	2.964	3.6	6.3	74.8	10.8	4.5
7	9	Editorial Essay........	2.899	2.9	8.3	64.5	10.6	13.7
8	3	Exposition............	2.888	4.3	4.5	67.4	11.7	12.1
9	6	Business Letter........	2.860	6.1	4.9	60.9	13.0	15.0
10	10	Debate Brief..........	2.767	3.6	5.4	56.0	17.1	18.0

Legend: B—5; NB—4; No Choice—3; NL—2; L—1

The Reliability of the Data

The same tests of reliability which were used with the composition title study were used with these data. The chance character of the returns was determined as in the former study. By chance it would

TABLE XLI

Rank Order List of Written Discourse Preferences by Eighth Grade

Rank	Title No.	Title	Median	Per Cent of Choices per Weight				
				5	4	3	2	1
		Boys and Girls						
1	5	Friendly Letter........	3.202	16.6	17.4	54.1	6.6	5.4
2	1	Narration.............	3.185	19.5	13.2	55.1	5.6	6.7
3	4	Argument.............	3.141	15.1	12.4	62.8	6.0	3.8
4	2	Description...........	3.124	12.2	14.6	62.0	6.7	4.6
5	8	News Article..........	3.003	6.7	8.0	71.0	9.4	4.9
6	3	Exposition............	2.955	6.6	6.5	67.8	9.6	9.5
7.5	6	Business Letter........	2.887	7.7	6.5	58.4	12.0	15.3
7.5	10	Debate Brief..........	2.887	5.8	8.5	58.2	16.1	11.4
9	9	Editorial Essay........	2.882	5.1	5.6	63.7	13.0	12.7
10	7	Poetry................	2.697	4.8	7.6	46.8	15.1	25.7
		Boys						
1	4	Argument.............	3.153	17.4	10.6	63.4	5.4	3.1
2	1	Narration.............	3.151	16.6	13.7	56.5	6.7	6.5
3	5	Friendly Letter........	3.144	11.7	17.9	57.5	6.7	6.2
4	2	Description...........	3.129	12.4	14.5	62.2	7.0	3.9
5	3	Exposition............	3.028	8.8	8.8	68.6	6.5	7.3
6	8	News Article..........	3.000	6.5	7.3	72.6	7.8	6.0
7	10	Debate Brief..........	2.903	7.5	9.8	54.7	16.8	11.1
8	6	Business Letter........	2.889	8.8	5.4	58.6	12.2	15.0
9	9	Editorial Essay........	2.872	4.9	4.9	64.0	14.0	12.2
10	7	Poetry................	2.505	5.4	7.0	42.0	16.8	28.8
		Girls						
1	5	Friendly Letter........	3.266	21.3	16.8	50.8	6.4	4.7
2	1	Narration.............	3.219	22.3	12.6	53.8	4.5	6.9
3	4	Argument.............	3.130	12.9	14.1	62.2	6.4	4.5
4	2	Description...........	3.120	11.9	14.6	61.9	6.4	5.2
5	8	News Article..........	3.006	6.9	8.7	69.6	10.9	4.0
6	9	Editorial Essay........	2.891	5.2	6.2	63.4	12.1	13.1
7	6	Business Letter........	2.886	6.7	7.4	58.4	11.9	15.6
8	3	Exposition............	2.884	4.5	4.2	67.1	12.6	11.6
9	10	Debate Brief..........	2.874	4.2	7.2	61.6	15.3	11.6
10	7	Poetry................	2.769	4.2	8.2	51.5	13.4	22.8

Legend: B—5; NB—4; No Choice—3; NL—2; L—1.

be expected that 20 per cent of the responses would be included in the B+NB or L+NL returns. The standard deviation for each list was determined by the formula, $\sigma_p \sqrt{\dfrac{pq}{N}}$. Then the range of 20

[*Text continued on page 78*]

TABLE XLII

RANK ORDER LIST OF WRITTEN DISCOURSE PREFERENCES BY NINTH GRADE

RANK	TITLE No.	TITLE	MEDIAN	PER CENT OF CHOICES PER WEIGHT				
				5	4	3	2	1
		Boys and Girls						
1	5	Friendly Letter........	3.216	17.8	17.2	52.8	6.6	5.6
2	2	Description..........	3.156	13.8	15.2	61.2	6.4	3.4
3	4	Argument............	3.141	14.5	13.3	61.9	5.9	4.4
4	1	Narration............	3.127	16.8	11.8	57.4	7.2	6.8
5	8	News Article.........	3.006	7.6	6.3	73.1	8.4	4.6
6	10	Debate Brief.........	2.964	7.8	10.0	60.0	12.7	9.5
7	3	Exposition...........	2.959	7.8	7.2	64.6	10.3	10.1
8	9	Editorial Essay.......	2.897	4.8	7.1	63.2	14.2	10.7
9	6	Business Letter.......	2.886	4.0	6.2	64.8	12.0	13.1
10	7	Poetry...............	2.548	5.1	5.8	41.1	16.1	31.9
		Boys						
1	1	Narration............	3.153	17.5	12.7	57.2	7.1	5.5
2.5	2	Description..........	3.136	12.0	15.7	61.3	7.6	3.5
2.5	4	Argument............	3.136	16.1	11.5	61.3	6.0	5.1
4	3	Exposition...........	3.082	12.4	10.6	64.5	7.1	5.3
5	5	Friendly Letter.......	3.074	10.6	14.8	57.8	9.2	7.6
6	8	News Article.........	3.010	8.5	6.2	71.9	9.9	3.5
7	10	Debate Brief.........	2.987	8.1	10.4	61.7	11.8	8.3
8	6	Business Letter	2.938	4.8	6.7	68.4	9.2	10.8
9	9	Editorial Essay.......	2.899	4.8	7.6	62.4	14.0	11.1
10	7	Poetry...............	2.090	5.1	3.9	33.6	18.0	39.4
		Girls						
1	5	Friendly Letter.......	3.400	25.4	19.8	47.4	3.9	3.4
2	2	Description..........	3.178	15.6	14.7	61.1	5.1	3.4
3	4	Argument............	3.146	12.7	15.2	62.6	5.9	3.7
4	1	Narration............	3.100	16.1	10.8	57.7	7.3	8.1
5	8	News Article.........	3.002	6.6	6.4	74.3	6.8	5.9
6	10	Debate Brief.........	2.937	7.6	9.5	58.4	13.7	10.8
7	9	Editorial Essay.......	2.895	4.6	6.6	64.0	14.4	10.3
8	3	Exposition...........	2.865	2.9	3.7	64.6	13.7	15.2
9	6	Business Letter.......	2.823	3.2	5.6	61.0	14.9	15.4
10	7	Poetry...............	2.742	5.1	7.8	48.9	14.2	24.0

Legend: B—5; NB—4; No Choice—3; NL—2; L—1.

TABLE XLIII
Rank Order List of Written Discourse Preferences by Tenth Grade

Rank	Title No.	Title	Median	Per Cent of Choices per Weight				
				5	4	3	2	1
		Boys and Girls						
1	5	Friendly Letter........	3.228	17.2	17.8	55.2	5.6	4.2
2	1	Narration.............	3.138	16.8	11.7	59.4	7.3	4.8
3	4	Argument.............	3.133	12.0	13.6	66.2	4.8	3.4
4	2	Description...........	3.116	13.5	11.5	65.4	5.9	3.8
5	8	News Article..........	3.020	6.7	7.3	75.1	7.3	3.6
6	10	Debate Brief..........	3.002	10.7	12.5	53.9	14.5	8.4
7	3	Exposition............	2.930	8.0	6.4	62.5	11.6	11.5
8	9	Editorial Essay........	2.918	6.5	6.9	63.0	13.5	10.0
9	6	Business Letter........	2.871	4.9	6.0	62.1	13.3	13.5
10	7	Poetry................	2.328	3.7	6.1	37.5	16.0	36.8
		Boys						
1	4	Argument.............	3.140	12.3	14.4	64.7	5.6	3.0
2	2	Description...........	3.104	12.8	11.2	65.6	6.4	4.0
3	1	Narration.............	3.102	16.1	10.4	59.0	9.0	5.6
4	5	Friendly Letter........	3.088	10.8	13.0	63.6	7.5	5.1
5	3	Exposition............	3.049	12.1	9.0	64.2	8.3	6.5
6	10	Debate Brief..........	3.044	10.9	15.3	52.1	14.0	7.7
7	8	News Article..........	3.042	8.6	8.2	72.6	7.3	3.4
8	9	Editorial Essay........	2.924	7.8	7.5	60.2	14.3	10.1
9	6	Business Letter........	2.919	6.2	6.5	64.2	12.2	10.9
10	7	Poetry................	1.903	2.3	4.5	33.9	15.5	43.8
		Girls						
1	5	Friendly Letter........	3.434	24.1	22.8	46.2	3.6	3.2
2	1	Narration.............	3.176	17.6	13.0	60.0	5.5	3.9
3	2	Description...........	3.135	14.3	11.9	64.6	5.4	3.6
4	4	Argument.............	3.126	11.6	13.0	67.8	3.9	3.7
5	8	News Article..........	2.999	4.7	6.4	77.7	7.3	3.9
6	10	Debate Brief..........	2.962	10.4	9.6	55.8	15.1	9.1
7	9	Editorial Essay........	2.912	5.1	6.2	65.8	13.0	9.8
8	6	Business Letter........	2.816	3.5	5.5	60.0	14.4	16.6
9	3	Exposition............	2.797	3.6	3.7	60.7	15.1	16.9
10	7	Poetry................	2.606	5.1	7.8	41.3	16.6	29.2

Legend: B—5; NB—4; No Choice—3; NL—2; L—1.

TABLE XLIV
Rank Order List of Written Discourse Preferences by Eleventh Grade

Rank	Title No.	Title	Median	Per Cent of Choices per Weight				
				5	4	3	2	1
		Boys and Girls						
1	4	Argument.............	3.160	14.0	13.8	65.4	3.6	3.2
2	5	Friendly Letter........	3.130	14.0	14.4	58.2	8.8	4.5
3	10	Debate Brief..........	3.112	10.8	18.7	52.6	9.9	7.9
4	1	Narration.............	3.103	15.8	9.5	62.3	6.5	5.9
5	2	Description...........	3.101	12.6	10.2	68.0	7.0	2.3
6	8	News Article..........	3.038	5.9	9.5	75.0	7.5	2.3
7	9	Editorial Essay........	2.993	9.9	9.0	61.2	11.5	8.3
8	3	Exposition............	2.904	8.3	5.9	60.1	14.9	10.8
9	6	Business Letter........	2.868	6.5	6.1	59.2	14.0	14.2
10	7	Poetry................	2.076	2.0	2.9	38.2	16.3	40.6
		Boys						
1	4	Argument.............	3.111	10.9	13.3	66.4	4.3	5.2
2	10	Debate Brief..........	3.103	9.5	20.4	50.7	11.4	8.1
3	1	Narration.............	3.085	17.5	7.1	61.2	9.0	5.2
4	8	News Article..........	3.059	7.1	10.9	72.5	7.1	2.4
5	2	Description...........	3.056	10.9	7.1	72.0	8.1	1.9
6	5	Friendly Letter........	3.046	10.4	11.8	61.2	10.4	6.2
7	9	Editorial Essay........	3.027	10.4	10.4	61.6	10.0	7.6
8	3	Exposition............	3.004	13.3	7.1	59.7	12.8	7.1
9	6	Business Letter........	2.951	8.1	7.6	62.6	13.3	8.5
10	7	Poetry................	1.655	1.9	4.3	32.2	13.7	47.9
		Girls						
1	5	Friendly Letter........	3.213	17.2	16.8	55.6	7.3	3.0
2	4	Argument.............	3.207	16.8	14.2	64.7	3.0	1.3
3	2	Description...........	3.144	14.2	12.9	64.2	6.0	2.6
4.5	1	Narration.............	3.119	14.2	11.6	63.4	4.3	6.5
4.5	10	Debate Brief..........	3.119	12.1	17.2	54.3	8.6	7.8
6	8	News Article..........	3.020	4.7	8.2	77.2	7.8	2.2
7	9	Editorial Essay........	2.961	9.5	7.8	60.8	12.9	9.1
8	3	Exposition............	2.814	3.9	4.7	60.4	16.8	14.2
9	6	Business Letter........	2.785	5.2	4.7	56.0	14.6	19.4
10	7	Poetry................	2.360	2.2	1.7	43.6	18.5	34.0

Legend: B—5; NB—4; No Choice—3; NL—2; L—1.

TABLE XLV
Rank Order List of Written Discourse Preferences by Twelfth Grade

Rank	Title No.	Title	Median	Per Cent of Choices per Weight				
				5	4	3	2	1
		Boys and Girls						
1	4	Argument............	3.268	23.2	12.9	59.8	3.3	.8
2	5	Friendly Letter........	3.187	12.9	17.0	64.3	3.7	2.1
3	10	Debate Brief..........	3.090	10.8	15.8	57.2	12.0	4.2
4	2	Description...........	3.085	14.9	8.7	63.5	10.0	2.9
5	8	News Article..........	3.081	8.7	10.0	74.7	4.2	2.5
6	1	Narration.............	3.038	11.2	10.8	60.6	12.9	4.6
7	9	Editorial Essay........	2.997	4.6	12.0	66.4	11.6	5.4
8	6	Business Letter........	2.904	4.2	7.1	65.1	13.3	10.4
9	3	Exposition............	2.895	7.9	5.0	61.4	14.1	11.6
10	7	Poetry................	1.493	2.9	.8	25.7	14.9	55.6
		Boys						
1	4	Argument............	3.263	21.3	13.9	62.3	1.6	.8
2	5	Friendly Letter........	3.125	9.0	16.4	65.6	6.6	2.5
3	8	News Article..........	3.076	9.8	8.2	75.4	5.7	.8
4	10	Debate Brief..........	3.070	11.5	10.6	64.8	9.8	3.3
5.5	2	Description...........	3.054	12.3	7.4	68.0	9.0	3.3
5.5	9	Editorial Essay........	3.054	4.9	18.0	60.6	11.5	4.9
7	3	Exposition............	3.034	12.3	9.0	61.4	10.6	6.6
8	1	Narration.............	2.972	13.1	5.7	59.0	18.9	3.3
9	6	Business Letter........	2.964	4.1	9.8	67.2	14.8	4.1
10	7	Poetry................	1.209	1.6	.8	15.6	11.5	70.5
		Girls						
1	4	Argument............	3.272	25.2	11.8	57.1	5.0	.8
2	5	Friendly Letter........	3.254	16.8	17.6	63.0	.8	1.7
3	10	Debate Brief..........	3.119	10.1	21.0	49.6	14.3	5.0
4	2	Description...........	3.113	16.8	10.1	59.6	10.9	2.5
5	1	Narration.............	3.086	7.6	16.0	63.8	6.7	5.9
6	8	News Article..........	3.085	7.6	11.8	74.0	2.5	4.2
7	9	Editorial Essay........	2.948	4.2	5.9	72.2	11.8	5.9
8	6	Business Letter........	2.840	4.2	4.2	63.0	11.8	16.8
9	3	Exposition............	2.753	3.4	.8	61.4	17.6	16.8
10	7	Poetry................	2.023	4.2	.8	36.1	18.5	40.3

Legend: B—5; NB—4; No Choice—3; NL—2; L—1.

per cent was found for each list. Those items falling within this range were considered chance returns. The following list contains the chance items found in all the lists:

Grade	Boys	Girls	Boys and Girls
7	Exposition	Poetry	
8		News Article	
9	Friendly Letter	Debate Brief	Debate Brief
10		Debate Brief	
11	Narration Friendly Letter Editorial Essay Exposition Business Letter	Editorial Essay	Editorial Essay
12	Friendly Letter Debate Brief Description Editorial Essay Exposition Narration Business Letter	Debate Brief Description Narration Editorial Essay	Debate Brief Description Narration Editorial Essay Exposition

A comparison of this list with Table XLVI indicates that the chance items on the boys and girls' list can be retained without changing the trends. This is true also for the girls, with the possible exception of the debate brief, though a decided trend is indicated—a trend seemingly supported by the chance returns. The boys' list is a trifle more complicated. The chance items in the seventh, eighth, ninth, and tenth grades are so scattered that they have no effect on the trends. There are too few cases in the eleventh and twelfth grades for any degree of certainty regarding choice, though it appears that the so-called chance items in these grades support the trends, except for Exposition and, possibly, Narration.

Here again, some variation in preferences would be expected from grade to grade, and this variation would be expected to be greatest between the most widely separated grades. In order to gain an indication of the degree of variability between the seventh and the other grades, the following rank-difference coefficients of correlation were obtained.

Written Discourse Preferences of High School Pupils

Grades Correlated	Boys	Girls	Boys and Girls
7–8	.90	.83	.92
7–9	.85	.74	.84
7–10	.92	.77	.87
7–11	.50	.62	.55
7–12	.57	.64	.48

TABLE XLVI
Rank Order List of Types of Composition Preferences (by Type Number) *

Rank	Boys Grade						Girls Grade						Boys and Girls Grade					
	7	8	9	10	11	12	7	8	9	10	11	12	7	8	9	10	11	12
1	4	4	1	4	4	4	5	5	5	5	5	4	5	5	5	5	4	4
2	2	1	2	2	10	5	1	1	2	1	4	5	1	1	2	1	5	5
3	5	5	4	1	1	8	2	4	4	2	2	10	2	4	4	4	10	10
4	1	2	3	5	8	10	4	2	1	4	1	2	4	2	1	2	1	2
5	3	3	5	3	2	2	7	8	8	8	10	1	8	8	8	8	2	8
6	8	8	8	10	5	9	8	9	10	10	8	8	3	3	10	10	8	1
7	9	10	10	8	9	3	9	6	9	9	9	9	9	6	3	3	9	9
8	6	6	6	9	3	1	3	3	3	6	3	6	6	10	9	9	3	6
9	10	9	9	6	6	6	6	10	6	3	6	3	7	9	6	6	6	3
10	7	7	7	7	7	7	10	7	7	7	7	7	10	7	7	7	7	7

* The horizontal lines in the columns divide the types above the median from those below it.

Types of Composition Used in Questionnaire I

1. Narration
2. Description
3. Exposition
4. Argument
5. Friendly Letter
6. Business Letter
7. Poetry
8. News Article suitable for a school newspaper
9. Editorial Essay suitable for a school newspaper
10. Debate Brief for either side of a debate

Analysis of the Lists

When boys' and girls' choices are combined, four types are seen to be preferred in all grades, in the following order of preference (the order is based on the average of positions in each grade): (1) Friendly Letter; (2) Argument; (3) Description; (4) Narration. Four dislikes are common to all grades, namely: (1) Poetry; (2) Business Letter; (3) Editorial Essay; (4) Exposition. No types are preferred in the lower grades and disliked in the upper grades. Writing the Debate Brief is distinctly disliked in the lower grades, but grows in preference as pupils pass through secondary schools until it becomes one of the most preferred types of written discourse. Writing the News Article is slightly disliked in the seventh grade and slightly liked in the others. For the most part, it remains in a neutral position.

One type of written discourse is liked by boys in all grades. It is Argumentation. Description and the Friendly Letter are liked through the tenth grade, though the evidence on the Friendly Letter is not conclusive in the ninth grade. The evidence on Exposition is not certain, but it appears to be a preference through the tenth grade. Their common dislikes in the order of most disliked first are: (1) Poetry; (2) Business Letter. Four types remain to be accounted for: narration is liked through the tenth grade, but not much can be said beyond that; the News Article holds a neutral position; the Editorial Essay is disliked in grades seven through ten—data for the eleventh and twelfth grades are inconclusive; we have noted how interest in writing the Debate Brief tends to increase as pupils reach the upper grades of the high school.

Four types of discourse are preferred by girls in all grades in the following order of preference: (1) Friendly Letter; (2) Argument; (3) Description; (4) Narration (the twelfth grade evidence is not conclusive for Description and Narration). Their dislikes in the order of most disliked first are as follows: (1) Poetry; (2) Exposition; (3) Business Letter; (4) Editorial Essay (through the tenth grade). News Article writing is colorless from the standpoint of interest, while there is apparently an increasing interest in the Debate Brief as girls reach the upper grades.

The likes and dislikes for boys and girls, combined in the separate grades, are given in the order in which they are most liked or most disliked to the extent that this is shown by the rank order lists.

PREFERENCES COMMON TO BOTH BOYS AND GIRLS BY GRADES

Grades

7	8	9	10	11	12
Friendly Letter	Friendly Letter	Friendly Letter	Friendly Letter	Argument	Argument
Narration	Narration	Description	Narration	Friendly Letter	Friendly Letter
Description	Argument	Argument	Argument	Debate Brief	News Article
Argument	Description	Narration	Description	Narration	
	News Article	News Article	News Article	Description	
			Debate Brief	News Article	

DISLIKES COMMON TO BOTH BOYS AND GIRLS BY GRADES

Grades

7	8	9	10	11	12
Debate Brief	Poetry	Poetry	Poetry	Poetry	Poetry
Poetry	Editorial Essay	Business Letter	Business Letter	Business Letter	Business Letter
Business Letter	Business Letter	Editorial Essay	Editorial Essay	Exposition	
Editorial Essay	Debate Brief	Exposition	Exposition	Editorial	
Exposition	Exposition	Debate Brief *		Essay *	
News Article					

* Items starred follow the trend but lack conclusive evidence.

To determine whether there are changes from liking a type in the lower grades to disliking it in the upper grades, or the reverse, the method of the standard error of the difference between two independent variables was used. This method reveals the types of discourse for which there is a distinct preference in one grade as compared to the other. The following preferences appear from the comparison of the seventh and twelfth grades:

	SEVENTH GRADE	TWELFTH GRADE
Boys and Girls................	Narration Poetry	Debate Brief
Boys.........................	Poetry	
Girls.........................	Poetry	Argument Debate Brief

SEX DIFFERENCES IN THE CHOICE OF TYPES OF DISCOURSE

As in the study of sex differences in topic interests, the method of the standard error of the difference between two independent variables was employed to determine the types of discourse for which there was a real difference in preference. The following differences were noted:

Boys		Girls	
Exposition......	All grades	Friendly Letter....	Grades 7, 9, 10
Argument......	Grade 7	Poetry...........	Grades 7, 9, 10
News Article....	Grade 10		

It seems evident, when boys and girls are compared, that if they are given a choice between using Exposition and the Friendly Letter, more boys than girls would select Exposition and more girls than boys would use the Friendly Letter. While girls are more likely than boys to prefer Poetry, it is more often the least preferred of the ten types of discourse by either boys or girls.

A second characteristic of sex differences for all grades (if we compare the tables of likes and dislikes) is that boys and girls reverse the order of their preferences, thus:

Boys	Girls
Argument	Friendly Letter
Narration	Narration
Description	Description
Friendly Letter	Argument

Conclusions

1. The Friendly Letter, Argument, Description, and Narration are the forms of written discourse liked in that order by the majority of all pupils in the secondary school grades.

2. Poetry, the Business Letter, the Editorial Essay, and Exposition are the forms of written discourse disliked in that order by the majority of all pupils in the secondary school grades.

3. Boys and girls agree closely in their likes and dislikes in all grades of the secondary schools when they are free to choose the types of written discourse which they prefer or dislike.

4. As pupils pass through the secondary school grades, they exhibit an increasing preference for the Debate Brief and Argument.

5. Sex differences appear in preferences for three topics. Exposition is preferred more by boys than by girls, while the Friendly Letter and Poetry are preferred more by girls than by boys.

6. There is a wide range in preferences and dislikes among all pupils. When boys and girls are considered either separately or

combined, it is true in all grades that each type of written discourse is both liked and disliked. Our rank order lists tend to show the preferences and the dislikes of the majority of pupils. Where it seems necessary to insist that one type of discourse be used for some particular purpose, it would seem that with a sufficiently wide range of topics to write about, pupils could find one which they would like to use for any given type of discourse.

CHAPTER VII

REVIEW OF CONCLUSIONS, WITH RECOMMENDATIONS FOR THEIR USE

The purpose of this summary is to indicate methods by which teachers may use these findings. To assume that their use automatically guarantees improvement in results, is to misunderstand the conception of interest upon which the study was made. Genuine interest secures spontaneous and concentrated attention. It secures continuity of effort. Although it does not necessarily reduce the amount of work to be done, it makes the work satisfying. It is accompanied by an attitude which is desirable for rapid, efficient learning. The interested pupil is more likely to make rapid progress, to learn economically and efficiently, to retain what he has learned. Interest leads to more complex activity, with a corresponding breadth of intellectual vision and recognition of needs for improvement. Under these conditions, it may be expected that interest in written composition will contribute to improvement in that activity.

How may the results of this study be used to secure interest in improvement? The psychology of interest makes it necessary to know the activities in which a pupil is already engaged, that is, his interests, and then to link the needed improvement to these activities as part of the development of facility in written composition. Dewey[1] defines good teaching as "teaching that appeals to established powers while it includes such *new* material as will demand their redirection for a new end, this redirection requiring thought—intelligent effort." This investigation was made in order to gain a more definite picture of the nature of pupils' interests to which the teacher might relate the new material to be learned. Our task now is to indicate certain techniques in teaching preferred in the light of our findings. The following recommendations are based upon pupils' interests, as revealed in the preceding chapters.

[1] Dewey, John, *Interest and Effort in Education*, p. 58. Riverside Educational Monographs. Houghton Mifflin Company, Boston, 1913.

The Assignment of Composition Topics

To attempt a redirection of present interests toward a new end, pupils should be permitted some latitude in choice of topics. Whether pupils write from topics of their own making or whether they select them from prepared lists, there is a marked variation in their choices. There is variation between the sexes, within each sex, and among boys and girls together in the same grade. While there are common likes (interests) within any given grade, they do not represent complete agreement of choice. All pupils do not like these topics. Therefore, an assignment intended to conform to pupils' interests would include a variety of specific topics. To give full play to interest, the assignment would permit writing on a topic suggested by the pupil; he may have a temporary interest about which he is eager to write.

The Relation of Pupils' Experience to Composition Topics

When pupils were asked why they chose a particular topic, more than half of them gave one of two reasons, either of which clearly indicated that the pupil had some special knowledge about the topic of his composition. Three other reasons for writing—Current Interest, Expectation, and Reading—are essentially the same; that is to say, pupils, when they choose topics for their compositions, write about topics within their experience. The practical question for the teacher, then, is to determine whether the topics she assigns are within the range of experience of her pupils—that is, whether they are too difficult or too abstract for them to handle. Our findings indicate two means of checking topics to conform with pupils' experience: in the first place, since the reasons were given when these topics were used as subjects for composition, the lists of interest are within pupils' experience, and the assignment of specific subjects within these categories insures reasonable certainty that pupils will know something about them. In the second place, the first fifteen classes of reasons give examples of types of experience which pupils have had. When topics are checked against these reasons, the per cent of pupils (within a grade) using a specific reason should be considered. For example, not many pupils say they write on account of their reading. Before they are asked to write on something connected with reading, it would be important to check the topics with their book lists.

Composition Topic Interests of Pupils

There are teachers today who, in assigning topics for written compositions, honestly attempt to offer topics which will interest pupils. In view of the lack of previous research, objective means for identifying interests have been limited. For the most part, the teacher has had to rely upon her own judgment to determine whether or not a topic fell within the range of the experience of her class, whether or not it was too dull. Whether a topic was too abstract or too difficult was a matter of subjective judgment. The lists of interests common to all grades provide an objective check for the topics in an assignment. It is not to be inferred that each assignment should include all the topics on any one list. On the contrary, until a pupil is launched on his interest in improvement, a series of assignments may be planned to explore his interests. A device especially adapted to the pupil whose interests are not easily discovered, would be the arrangement of several lists of titles, each including the categories of interest presented here. In concluding this discussion, it seems worth while to suggest that, since interests peculiar to a given group or locality will serve to motivate a desire for improvement, teachers will want to supplement the lists given here with their local interests.

Check Lists of Interests Common to All Grades

Boys and Girls	Boys	Girls
Travel	Travel	Travel
Adventure	Outdoor Activities	Adventure
Outdoor Activities	Athletics and Sports	Personal Experience
Ethics	Adventure	Outdoor Activities
Athletics and Sports	Current Events	Ethics
Personal Experience	Ethics	Literature
Literature	Machines	Animals
Humorous Anecdotes	Famous People	Humorous Anecdotes
Sympathy	Leisure Activities	Sympathy
Animals	Pupil Employment	Getting Rich
Home Life	Animals	Leisure Activities
Pupil Employment	Getting Rich	Pupil Employment
Leisure Activities	Literature	Religion
Current Events	Aviation*	Sports*
Famous People	Personal Experience*	
Getting Rich	School*	
Vocations*		

* Starred items are taken from Free Choice Composition Lists.

CHECK LISTS OF INTERESTS LIKED BY ONE SEX AND DISLIKED BY THE OTHER

Likes

Boys	Girls
Athletics and Sports	Animals
Current Events	Humorous Anecdotes
Famous People	Literature
Leisure Activities	Personal Experience
Machines	Sympathy
Pupil Employment	

Dislikes

Fairy Tales	Machines
Proverbs	People
Religion	Historical Events
	Modern Industries

Pupils' Interests in Types of Discourse

For the teacher who would explore the interests of her class in the various types of discourse, the lists of pupils' interests give definite information. The majority of boys and girls prefer (1) the Friendly Letter, (2) Argument, (3) Description, and (4) Narration in that order. The only exception is that girls show slight preference for exposition, also. Most pupils may be expected to prefer these types of discourse. Most pupils are indifferent about the News Article, but definitely dislike writing Poetry, a Business Letter, or an Editorial Essay. Ordinarily, the last three types would not be assigned with the expectation that a majority of pupils would produce satisfactory work.

This summary discloses a need, the fulfillment of which will aid materially in the definite use of the interests revealed in this study. Their usefulness will be increased when further research has revealed the effect of each topic or type of discourse upon facility and general merit in written composition.

APPENDIX I

DIRECTIONS FOR RANKING THESE LISTS OF TITLES

Each list contains ten titles. Each numbered heading describes the general topic to which the titles belong. It is proposed to offer to pupils of the junior and senior high school grades titles from each general heading for the purpose of ascertaining what these pupils like to write about. You are asked to select the best five titles in each heading on the following bases:

I. The accuracy with which any given title is related to its general (numbered) heading; that is, if a pupil uses a certain title, can it be said with reasonable assurance that he is writing about the topic of the general heading?

II. The suitability of any given title in so far as the general topic is common experience for pupils of both sexes, ranging from the seventh through the twelfth grade (approximately the ages of twelve to eighteen).
  A. Some criteria of suitability:
    1. Does the title suggest experience common to practically all pupils, whether from the city or from the rural districts?
    2. Does the title appeal to both sexes?
    3. Will the meaning of the title be understood by all pupils?
    4. Is the title a reasonably good one about which to write a composition?
    5. Which titles make the best appeal to the youngest as well as the oldest pupil in our category?

Place a number 1 at the left of the best title in each heading, a number 2 at the left of the second best, and so on for the five best titles in each general topic.

1. *Adult Occupations or Vocations:* Occupations or vocations in which adults engage.
   How I Expect to Earn My Living
   The Best Preparation for a Business (or some other) Career
   Qualifications for a Good Stenographic (or some other) Position
   An Interview with a Farmer on Farming as a Business (or some other man or woman about some other business)
   Why I Hope to Be a Journalist (or whatever you hope to be)
   The Medical (or some other) Profession as a Life Work
   Choosing a Profession
   What an Engineer (or some other worker) Has to Do
   Why I Think I Would Make a Good (name some occupation)
   Duties of a Storekeeper (or some other worker)

2. *Adventure:* In which danger, daring, mystery, or some other excitement is the central theme.
   The Ninth Inning, Bases Full, Score Tied, and None Out

Adventures in a Deserted House
An Exciting Race
A Fight with Indians
When the Circus Lions Broke Out
The Phantom Airplane
Caught in a Storm
From a Cyclone Cellar
Adrift on a Raft
When We Won the Championship Game

3. *Animals:* Any kind.
    A Good Dog for Children
    Points of a Good Horse
    How to Train a Dog
    Taking Care of a Pet
    How My Dog Shows His Feelings
    A Jersey Cow
    A Fox Terrier
    An Angora Cat
    A Carrier Pigeon
    Why I Like an Animal for a Pet

4. *Art:* Includes painting, freehand drawing, sculpture, design, etching, modeling, and wood- and linoleum-cutting.
    A Picture I Would Like to Own
    Making a Woodcut (or a Linoleum Print)
    A Statue I Admire
    An Old Painting
    Some Objects at the Art Museum Worth Going to See
    The Beauties of the Lincoln Memorial in Washington, D. C.
    What Is Meant by Balance in Design
    My Favorite Picture
    How to Appreciate Art
    Some of the Beautiful Buildings in Our City

5. *Athletics and Sports:* Includes all organized or team games.
    Why I Like to Play Football (or some other team game)
    How to Serve in Tennis
    Laying Out a Baseball Diamond
    The Development of Football
    Basketball Is More (or Less) Interesting than Football
    How to Play Baseball (or some other team game)
    The Greatest American Sport
    Why Every Pupil Should Play on Some School Team
    Benefits from Playing on an Athletic Team
    Tennis Is More Valuable than Football

6. *Children:* Those younger than the pupils using the title for a composition.
    The Cutest Thing Our Baby Does
    Stories Little Children Like to Hear
    What I Enjoy About Taking Care of Babies

Appendix

    Teaching Baby a New Trick
    Proper Care of Babies
    How a Baby Learns to Walk
    Interesting Habits of Babies
    Some New Words Our Baby Has Learned
    My Baby Brother (or Sister)
    The Tyrant—A Baby

7. *Civics:* Problems of government.
    How Our Town (or City) Is Governed
    How a City Pays Its Bills
    Why Stamps Are Used on Letters
    The Process of Obtaining a Patent from the Government
    Why There Are Two Houses of Congress
    It Is the Duty of a Good Citizen to Vote
    How Good Roads Help the Farmer
    How the President Is Elected
    What the Mayor Has to Do
    Different Forms of City Government Today

8.* *Contemporaneous Famous People:* Any living individual.
    Babe Ruth
    Jane Addams
    Mrs. Lindbergh (or Thomas A. Edison)
    Henry Ford (or Mrs. Coolidge)
    Herbert Hoover (or Alfred E. Smith)
    Colonel Lindbergh (or Amelia Earhart)
    Booth Tarkington
    Sinclair Lewis
    Ambassador Dwight Morrow

9. *Current Events:* Noteworthy happenings of the immediate present.
    The Flights of the Graf Zeppelin Across the Atlantic
    The Recent Presidential Election
    The Investigation of the Power Trust
    The Present Session of Congress
    The New China
    The Kellogg Anti-War Treaties
    Latest Attempts to Settle the World War Reparations Problems
    The New American Judge of the World Court, Charles E. Hughes
    The American-Supervised Election in Nicaragua
    Commander Byrd's South Pole Expedition

10. *Ethics:* Having to do with standards of conduct.
    My Ideal Man (or Woman)
    The Honor System in Examinations
    A Schoolmate Who Borrows
    The Right Kind of Chum
    Why It Pays to Be Honest

* One name omitted because the names Herbert Hoover and Alfred E. Smith originally were listed separately.

Why Tale-Bearers Are Disliked
Good Sportsmanship in Games
A Good Turn
It is Wrong for a Boy to Tease His Sister
Some Marks of a Lady (or a Gentleman)
11. *Fairy Tales and Legends:* Any fairy tale or legend.
A Fairy Tale I Like
An Old Legend
The Story of the Golden Fleece
A Modern Fairy Tale
King Arthur and His Court
Indian Legends
Fairy Tales Every Child Should Know
My Favorite Fairy Tale
Legends About the Stars Which I Like
A Story from Andersen's Fairy Tales
12. *Getting Rich:* Central theme concerned with having or obtaining wealth.
What I Would Do with a Million Dollars
Why I Want to Be Rich
How Carnegie (or some other rich man) Made His Fortune
How to Make Money in Advertising (or some other position)
Inventions That Have Made Men Wealthy
From Poor Boy to Rich Man
How I Expect to Become Rich
The Responsibility of Being Rich
Short Roads to Wealth
Why I Would Like to Be Rich
13. *Handwork:* The process of doing some piece of handwork.
How to Make Punch Work (or a Bow and Arrow)
How to Make an Apron (or a Book Rack)
How to Make a Cake (or a Kite)
How to Set a Table for a Formal Dinner (or Make a Radio)
How to Make a Jointed Toy (or a Hat)
How to Make a Mince Pie (or an Airplane)
How to Harness a Horse (or Make Fudge)
How to Play (some game you like)
How to Pack a Traveling Bag
How to Drive an Automobile
14. *Health:* Any phase of personal or public health or of physiology with which the pupil may be familiar.
First Aid Lessons for Beginners
How the Heart Works
On Eating Candy Between Meals
The Value of Regular Sleeping Habits
The Filthy Fly
How to Give Artificial Respiration
How Medical Inspection Helps Pupils

Appendix

      How to Use a Triangular Bandage
      Some Simple Good Health Rules
      The Good Health Side of Athletics
15. *Historic Events, Sites, or Characters:*
      The Boston Tea Party
      Famous Discoveries of the Fifteenth Century
      Medieval Trade Guilds
      My Hero (or Heroine) in History
      An Important Historical Event
      The Battle of the Marne (or some other great battle)
      The Making of Our Flag
      The Discovery of Gold in California
      What the Crusades Were
      Some Person Famous in History, such as Daniel Boone, Florence Nightingale, or Napoleon
16. *Home Life or Participation by the Pupil in Home Life:*
      My Duty to My Home
      Electric Appliances Which Make Housework Easy
      Helping Father (or Mother)
      My Ideal House
      Improving Our Backyard
      Putting the Garage in Order
      Putting the Living Room in Order
      Polishing the Silver (or Looking After the Furnace)
      What Home Ought to Be
      Home Is Something More Than a House
17. *Humorous Anecdotes:* Stories or incidents.
      The Funniest Story I Ever Heard
      A Joker Joked
      A Funny Incident at School
      A Surprise for Surprisers
      Where I Find Funny Stories to Tell
      A Humorous Mishap
      The Biggest Fish Story I Ever Heard
      Embarrassing Moments That Were Funny
      How to Tell Funny Stories
      A Joke We Played on (some one)
18. *Indefinite Titles:* No definite kind of composition is suggested by the **title**.
      Never Again!
      A Bad Bargain
      A Hundred Years from Now
      A Fighting Failure
      How a Story Grows
      Moving Days
      A Brave Deed
      A Long Five Minutes
      Fired!
      Burned Biscuits

19. *Leisure Activities:* Any pleasurable activity of the pupils which is not classified elsewhere on the list.
    My Favorite Amusement
    The Movie I Like Best
    Why I Like the Campfire Girls (or Girl Scouts or Boy Scouts)
    A Good Game to Play at a Mixed Party
    Halloween Sports
    Rare Stamps in My Collection
    My First Autograph Album
    A Collection I Have Made
    The Fun There Is in a Hobby
    Why Chess (or something else) Is My Hobby
20. *Literature:* Any feature of books, poetry, or literary articles which pupils have read.
    The Book I Liked Best
    A Cowboy I Met in a Book
    Why I Did (Not) Like (some book)
    Poems I Like to Read Over Again
    Modern Story Writers
    The Greatest American Author (or Poet)
    A Good Book
    My Opinion of Tom Sawyer (or some other character in a book)
    My Best Friend in a Book
    The Kind of Books I Enjoy Most
21. *Machines:* Descriptions or qualities of the mechanism of any machine.
    The Points of a Good Bicycle
    Advantages of the Air-Cooled Motor in Aviation
    A Cotton Baling Machine
    How a Gasoline Engine Works
    Designing Special Machines for Special Work
    Automobiles, Past and Present
    Dirigible Balloons
    How a Reaper Works
    The Inside of a Submarine
    How a Pump Works
22. *Modern Industries:* Any phase of the process or physical equipment of any modern industry.
    A Visit to a Glass Factory (or some other kind of factory)
    The Printing of a Modern Newspaper
    Passenger Air Service in the United States Today
    The Chief Industry of Our Town
    The Sugar Industry of America
    How Coffee Is Grown
    How Rubber Is Obtained
    How Maple Sugar Is Made
    How Paper Is Made
    How Shoes Are Made

23. *Music:* Any phase.
   My Favorite Musical Instrument
   Music—The Greatest Contribution of Modern Times to Civilization
   Learning to Play the Piano (or some other musical instrument)
   My Feelings When Listening to a Great Musician
   Why I Like to Hear Galli-Curci (or some other famous singer)
   My Favorite Musical Composer
   Listening to a Symphony Orchestra
   Why I Like Jazz
   Some Records for a Permanent Phonograph Library
   Possibilities of the Player Piano
24. *Outdoor Activities:* Excluding organized or team athletics.
   Swimming (or some other sport which can be played without a team) Is My Favorite Sport
   The Best Winter Sport
   Simple Rules for Making Camp Overnight
   Sailing a Boat
   Bicycling
   One of the Best Hikes I Ever Took
   Marks of an Able Canoeist
   A Dinner in the Woods
   Cooking Dinner on a Hike
   Standard Equipment for Hikers
25. *People:* Character studies or descriptions of appearance.
   The Old Soldier
   Our Doctor
   A Very Little Girl
   The Organ Grinder
   A Beautiful Lady
   The Old Judge
   The Waitress
   The Auctioneer
   The Umpire
   The Barker at the Side-Show
26. *Personal Experience:* In which the pupil talks about **himself**.
   My First Formal Party
   My Feelings When My Themes Are Read in Class
   My Own Biography
   A Day I Shall Never Forget
   My First Race (or Basketball Game, etc.)
   A Temptation Which I Resisted
   The Pleasantest Day of My Vacation
   When I Had Measles
   My First Circus
   When I Was Very Young
27. *Proverbs:*
   Silence Is Golden

A Stitch in Time Sometimes Saves Nine
Too Many Cooks Spoil the Broth
Well Begun is Half Done
Birds of a Feather Flock Together
Where There's a Will There's a Way
A Friend in Need Is a Friend Indeed
A Small Leak Will Sink a Great Ship
One To-day Is Worth Two To-morrows
Little Strokes Fell Great Oaks

28. *Pupil Employment for Financial Remuneration:* After-school jobs or other methods of earning money while attending school.
    How I Earn My Spending Money
    After-School Jobs for Girls (or Boys) to Earn Money
    My First Business Venture
    Selling (or Distributing) Papers
    Ways in Which Some of My School Friends Earn Money
    Working Your Way Through School
    Some Odd Jobs I Have Done for Pay
    How One Boy (or Girl) Earned Money Through a Hobby
    Interesting Part-Time Jobs
    Summer Jobs for School Pupils

29. *Religion:* Church, religious organizations, Bible study, or religious history.
    What Church Means to Me
    Our Sunday School Class
    A Sermon I Heard on a Recent Sunday
    Values One May Derive from Bible Study
    The Value of the Girl Reserves (or Hi-Y) to Its Members
    Why I Like to Listen to Dr. Fosdick (or some other preacher)
    Why I Am a Presbyterian (or whatever your religion is)
    What Religion Means to Me
    Why I Go to Sunday School
    The Great Religions of the World

30. *School:* Any phase, curricular or extra-curricular, where the central theme is the school.
    The Best Way to Study Lessons
    The Classes I Like Best at School
    What It Means to Be Loyal to Our School
    Examination Week, or Cramming
    How Student Meetings Should Be Run
    A Practical Use of Geometry
    Too Much Home Work
    Why Pupils Quit School
    School Should Be Open the Year Round
    The School Club I Belong To

31. *Science:* Anything included in classes in the school in General Science, or any phase of the specific Physical or Natural Science Courses.
    Why Yeast Raises Dough

An Eclipse—What It Is
A Wonder Seen Through a Microscope
How a Dynamo Works
Why Birds Migrate
The Scum on Our Pond
An Ant I Watched (or Read About)
Adventures of an Amateur Naturalist
What Causes Lightning and Thunder
Some Trees I Know

32. *Sentiment:* Love for or interest in someone of the opposite sex.
    When I Thought I Was in Love
    My First Beau (or Girl)
    What I Know About Girls (or Boys)
    The First Time I Escorted a Girl Home (or Was Escorted Home by a Boy)
    How an Old Letter Revived an Old Love Affair
    Asking Her Father's Consent
    Buying a Gift for a Boy (or a Girl)
    Why I Read Love Stories
    Why Boys and Girls Should Attend the Same School
    It Is a Good Practice to Have a Steady Girl (or Boy) Friend

33. *Social Problems:* Problems pertaining to society or its organization.
    One Solution of the High Cost of Living Problem
    A Reformer and His Work
    Hull House, Chicago (or the Salvation Army or similar organizations)
    It Is Unwise to Feed Tramps
    Employment for Men Out of Work
    The Tragedy of Poverty
    The Junior Red Cross
    Congress Should Create Old Age Pensions for All Citizens
    One Central Organization to Handle All Poor Relief Has Advantages

34. *Sympathy:* Sympathy or kindness toward some person or animal.
    How Two Poor Children Were Made Happy
    It Pays to Be Kind
    Memorial Day Is Our Most Sacred Holiday
    Courtesies We Owe to Elderly People
    Why I Believe in the Society for the Prevention of Cruelty to Animals
    What Visits and Flowers Mean to Invalids
    When It Is Kind to Kill Animals
    Ways in Which Animals Show Appreciation
    The Reward of a Kind Deed
    Kindness—The Mark of a Gentleman

35. *Travel:* Places to visit or places visited.
    A Trip I Would Like to Take
    A Visit to Washington, D. C.
    Visiting Yellowstone National Park
    Places Worth Seeing in England (or some other country)
    A Ride to Mount Vernon

A Trip to Alaska
Our Trip to (some place you have visited)
How People Live in Holland (or some other country)
Why I Want to Travel
What I Would Like to See in Europe (or some other place)

36. *Winning Prizes:* Any phase of winning medals, letters, or other prizes.
The Prize I Think the Most Of
Why I Want to Win (name some prize)
What It Means to Win Our School Emblem
Why Beauty Contests Are Interesting
Is Prize-Winning Noble?
A Brave Deed Which Won a Medal
Why Brave Soldiers (or Policemen or Firemen) Are Given Medals
A Prize I Would Like to Have Won
One Prize Which Was Worthy to Be Given
Some Persons Who Have Won the Congressional Medal

APPENDIX II

COMPOSITION INVESTIGATION

General Directions to Teachers

Your cooperation is solicited for these questionnaires. They are being used as a part of an investigation to discover some of the topics pupils like to write about. The work you are asked to do has been planned to use but a minimum of your time. The results of the investigation will be made available for you as soon as they have been printed. The materials are to be used as described below:

Order of use:
1. Questionnaire I may be given at any time which is convenient.
2. The rest of the materials should be given in the following order:

>The Free Choice Composition
>Assignment of List A
>Assignment of List B
>Assignment of List C

Pupils have not been asked to write their names on any questionnaire. The reason for omitting the names is to leave pupils free to make whatever choices they desire. It is necessary, however, to be able to identify all of each pupil's work. To that end will you give each pupil in each class a number which he will use on each item he makes out. The number should be on the questionnaire when it is distributed. If desirable, some trustworthy pupil might do this work of numbering the questionnaires. Do not return a key list with the questionnaires.

Directions for the Free Choice Composition

For the first assignment have each pupil write one composition. He will choose his own title, being free to write upon any topic he desires. When the compositions are handed in, tabulate the numbers and titles on the Free Choice Composition blanks, one blank for each class. Your name is desired on this page (and in a few other places later) solely for purposes of identifying all materials; your name will not be used in any other way in this entire investigation.

Directions for Questionnaire I

Have each pupil fill out one questionnaire. Be sure he has done all that is asked of him. Choices should be indicated *in front of* each number. Pay no attention to either the titles of these questionnaires or to their number arrangement. Simply pass them out in the order in which they have been handed to you. Collect them as soon as they have been filled out and tie them in a pile, placing your name and the grade on a slip on top of the pile. Make certain that each questionnaire has each pupil's key number on it.

DIRECTIONS FOR USING LISTS A, B, AND C

1. Each list is to be used for a separate assignment, preferably one a week. Use list A first, B second, and C last. Have each list numbered before it is distributed. Do not hand out one list until the preceding one is completed and returned to you.
2. You will find that the number arrangement on any one list varies. This is intentional. When you hand out a set, do not attempt to rearrange the separate sheets but distribute them as they are, taking one from the top of the pile each time.
3. When you distribute a list, announce that for the next written assignment each pupil is to choose the title for his composition from this particular list. Where there is a parenthesis in a title, the pupil may do whatever is indicated within the parenthesis. The stub at the bottom of the list is to be handed in with the composition. In addition to the questions asked on the stub, have each pupil write his answer to the following question on the back of the stub: *Why did you choose the title you did?*
4. When all three sets of stubs are collected, kindly tie them up in piles so that the three slips from each pupil are in the same pile. Make one pile for each class. Place your name on a slip on top of the pile.
5. It is important that these compositions should not be read or corrected publicly or in any way that would embarrass a pupil on account of his choice of title.
6. If you find it convenient, arrangements will be made to collect all the compositions from you when you have finished with them.

TITLES FOR COMPOSITIONS

1. How I Expect to Earn My Living
2. Caught in a Storm
3. Taking Care of a Pet
4. My Favorite Picture
5. Why Every Pupil Should Play on Some School Team
6. The Tyrant—A Baby
7. How Our Town (or City) Is Governed
8. Colonel Lindbergh (or Amelia Earhart)
9. The Flights of the Graf Zeppelin Across the Atlantic

10. The Right Kind of Chum
11. An Old Legend
12. What I Would Do with a Million Dollars
13. How to Play (some game you like)
14. First Aid Lessons for Beginners
15. My Hero (or Heroine) in History
16. Helping Father (or Mother)
17. The Funniest Story I Ever Heard
18. Never Again!

19. My Favorite Amusement
20. The Book I Like Best
21. Automobiles, Past and Present
22. A Visit to a Glass Factory (or some other kind of factory)
23. My Favorite Musical Instrument
24. The Best Winter Sport
25. The Old Soldier
26. A Day I Shall Never Forget
27. A Friend in Need Is a Friend Indeed

28. How I Earn My Spending Money
29. Why I Go to Sunday School
30. The Class (or Classes) I Like Best at School
31. An Eclipse—What It Is
32. Why Boys and Girls Should Attend the Same School
33. It is Unwise to Feed Tramps
34. Courtesies We Owe to Elderly People
35. A Trip I Would Like to Take
36. A Prize I Would Like to Have Won

(A)   No............

TO THE PUPIL:

From this list of titles for compositions you are asked to choose one title for your next composition. Look the entire list over before you make your choice. Where there is a parenthesis, you may substitute whatever is in it for the words already in the title. After you have made your selection, fill in the information asked for below. Then tear off this slip and hand it to your teacher when you hand in your composition.

Boy...... Girl......   Grade in school (draw a circle around your grade)

                                         7   8   9   10   11   12

Age last birthday......yrs.

     The title for my composition is number...............................
     The title I like next best is number...................................
     The title I like least (dislike most) is number.........................
     The title I like next least is number.................................

TITLES FOR COMPOSITIONS

10. Good Sportsmanship in Games
11. An Indian Legend
12. Inventions That Have Made Men Wealthy
13. How to Set a Table for a Formal Dinner (or Make a Radio)
14. Some Simple Good Health Rules
15. An Important Historical Event
16. Electric Appliances Which Make Housework Easy
17. Embarrassing Moments That Were Funny
18. A Long Five Minutes

19. The Movie I Like Best
20. The Kind of Books I Enjoy Most
21. Dirigible Balloons
22. The Printing of a Modern Newspaper
23. Why I Like (or Dislike) Jazz
24. One of the Best Hikes I Ever Took
25. The Umpire
26. The Pleasantest Day of My Vacation
27. A Stitch in Time Sometimes Saves Nine

28. Some Odd Jobs I Have Done for Pay
29. Our Sunday School Class
30. What It Means to Be Loyal to Our School
31. Adventures of an Amateur Naturalist
32. Why I Read Love Stories
33. The Tragedy of Poverty
34. Ways in Which Animals Show Appreciation
35. Why I Want to Travel
36. The Prize I Think the Most Of

1. Why I Think I Would Make a Good (name some occupation)
2. Adventure in a Deserted House
3. Why I Like an Animal for a Pet
4. Some of the Beautiful Buildings in Our City
5. The Greatest American Sport
6. My Baby Brother (or Sister)
7. It Is the Duty of a Good Citizen to Vote
8. Henry Ford (or Mrs. Coolidge)
9. Commander Byrd's South Pole Expedition

(B)　　　　　　　　　　　No............

To THE PUPIL:

From this list of titles for compositions you are asked to choose one title for your next composition. Look the entire list over before you make your choice. Where there is a parenthesis you may substitute whatever is in it for the words already in the title. After you have made your selection, fill in the information asked for below. Then tear off this slip and hand it to your teacher when you hand in your composition.

Boy...... or Girl......　　Grade in school (draw a circle around your grade)
　　　　　　　　　　　　　　　　7　8　9　10　11　12

Age last birthday......yrs.

　　The title for my composition is number...............................
　　The title I like next best is number..
　　The title I like least (dislike most) is number...........................
　　The title I like next least is number.....................................

TITLES FOR COMPOSITIONS

19. A Collection I Have Made (Stamps or Butterflies, etc.)
20. My Opinion of Tom Sawyer (or some other character in a book)
21. How a Gasoline Engine Works
22. The Chief Industry of Our Town
23. Listening to a Symphony (or some other) Orchestra
24. Simple Rules for Making Camp Overnight
25. Our Doctor
26. My Feelings When My Themes Are Read in Class
27. Too Many Cooks Spoil the Broth

28. Summer Jobs for School Pupils
29. The Value of the Girl Reserves (or Hi-Y) to Its Members
30. Why Pupils Quit School
31. Why Birds Migrate
32. Buying a Gift for a Boy (or a Girl)
33. The Junior Red Cross
34. What Visits and Flowers Mean to Invalids
35. What It Means to Win Our School Emblem
36. Our Trip to (some place you have visited)

1. Why I Hope to Be a Journalist (or whatever you hope to be)
2. An Exciting Race
3. How a Dog Shows His Feelings
4. A Statue I Admire
5. Benefits from Playing on an Athletic Team
6. The Cutest Thing Our Baby Does
7. Why Stamps Are Used on Letters
8. Babe Ruth
9. President-Elect Hoover's South American Trip
10. A Good Turn
11. A Fairy Tale I Like
12. Why I Would Like to Be Rich
13. How to Make Mince Pie (or an Airplane)
14. The Filthy Fly
15. Some Person Famous in History, such as: Daniel Boone, Florence Nightingale, or Napoleon
16. My Ideal House
17. A Funny Incident
18. A Bad Bargain

(C)   No..........

To the Pupil:

From this list of titles for compositions you are asked to choose one title for your next composition. Look the entire list over before you make your choice. Where there is a parenthesis you may substitute whatever is in it for the words already in the title. After you have made your selection, fill in the information asked for below. Then tear off this slip and hand it to your teacher when you hand in your composition.

Boy...... or Girl......   Grade in school (Draw a circle around your grade)

Age last birthday......yrs.   7   8   9   10   11   12

    The title for my composition is number................................
    The title I like next best is number......................................
    The title I like least (dislike most) is number..........................
    The title I like next least is number....................................

APPENDIX III

SAMPLES OF TYPES OF DISCOURSE QUESTIONNAIRES

QUESTIONNAIRE 1A

To the Pupils:　　　　　　　　　　　　　　　　　　　　No............

　Please fill in the spaces below.

Boy or Girl......... Age last birthday......... Grade in school.........

Directions

Suppose you are required to write something about winter. In which of the following ways would you prefer to write? The title must have something in it about winter, but if you would like to write in some particular way suggested below on a topic about winter different from the one suggested, that would be satisfactory. Read the entire list through carefully before you decide. Then do what the directions at the bottom of the page tell you to do.

1. Make up a story about winter or about something that happened in winter.
2. Describe how something—perhaps a city or hill—looks in winter.
3. Explain why there is a winter season, why snow is formed, or something similar.
4. Give some reasons why you like or dislike winter.
5. Write a letter to a friend about something interesting you have done or seen in winter.
6. Write a letter on some such topic as ordering a supply of fuel for heating a house in winter or asking some architect for information about various methods of heating houses.
7. Write a poem about winter, winter scenes, or things which happen in winter.
8. Write a news article suitable for a school newspaper about some winter event or sport at your school.
9. Write an editorial suitable for a school newspaper on some topic such as: Winter Sports Which Could Be Introduced at Our School, or Winter Sports for Girls, or Flooding the School Playground for Ice Skating.
10. Write an argument for or against something about winter such as: Winter Sports Are Better Than Summer Sports, or The City Should Prohibit **Traffic on Some Hill Streets to Provide for Coasting.**

(a) Write a B in front of the one you like best.
(b) Write NB in front of the one you like next best.
(c) Write an L in front of the one you like least (dislike most).
(d) Write NL in front of the one you like next least.

QUESTIONNAIRE 1B

To the Pupil: No............
Please fill in the spaces below.
Boy or Girl......... Age last birthday......... Grade in school.........

Directions

Suppose you are required to write something about airplanes or aviators or some unusual airplane flights. In which of the following ways would you prefer to write? The title must have something in it about airplanes, but if you would like to write in some particular way suggested, that would be satisfactory. Read the entire list through carefully before you decide. Then do what the directions at the bottom of the page tell you to do.

6. Write a letter asking for a time-table from some airway company or inquiring about purchasing a plane or working for an aircraft manufacturer.
7. Write a poem about some aviator, some flight, or something else concerned with airplanes.
8. Write a news article suitable for a school newspaper on some such topic as: Some Aviator (who may have visited your school or city), an Airplane Flight, an Airplane Show, or an Airport.
9. Write an editorial suitable for a school newspaper about some such topic as: Why Our School Should Have a Course in Aeronautics, Inspiring Deeds of Aviators, or Why Our City Needs an Airport.
10. Write an argument for or against some topic concerned with aviation, such as: Airplanes Will Replace Passenger Trains, or The Airplane Has a Better Future Than the Dirigible.
1. Make up a story in which something about aviation is a part of the story.
2. There are different kinds of airplanes. Describe how some plane looks on the ground or in flight.
3. Explain how an airplane works, or how some special device is used on airplanes.
4. Give some reasons why airplanes are especially useful for some special purpose, such as: carrying mail, war, or trade.
5. Write a letter to a friend telling about some incident connected with airplanes, such as: a ride, an accident, or some noted flier.

(a) Write a B in front of the one you like best.
(b) Write NB in front of the one you like next best.
(c) Write an L in front of the one you like least (dislike most).
(d) Write NL in front of the one you like next least.

QUESTIONNAIRE 1c

To the Pupil: No............
 Please fill in the spaces below.
 Boy or Girl......... Age last birthday......... Grade in school.........

Directions

Suppose you are required to write something about games—party games, athletic games, indoor games, outdoor games, or any other kind you can think of. In which of the following ways would you prefer to write? The title must have something in it about games, but if you would like to write in some particular way suggested below on a topic about games different from the one suggested, that would be satisfactory. Read the entire list through carefully before you decide. Then do what the directions at the bottom of the page tell you to do.

1. Make up a story about a game or use a game as the basis for a story.
2. Suppose some game or tournament is being played. Describe what might be seen.
3. Explain the rules for playing some game, such as: basketball (for boys or girls), chess, charades, etc.
4. Give some reasons why you like or dislike some game, either a social or athletic game.
5. Write a letter to a friend telling about some game you saw or played in.
6. Write a letter ordering equipment with which to play some game or making arrangements to play some game with some other class or school.
7. Write a poem using something about games for the topic.
8. Write a news article suitable for a school newspaper about some school game.
9. Write an editorial suitable for a school newspaper upon some topic such as: Some Marks of Good Sportsmanship, The Value of Competitive Games to a School (or to a Player), or Some Desirable Changes in Our Eligibility Rules for School Athletics and Contests.
10. Write some arguments for or against games on some such topic as: One Should Always Play to Win, Coaches are Expensive Luxuries, or Social Games are a Waste of Time.

(a) Write a B in front of the one you like best.
(b) Write NB in front of the one you like next best.
(c) Write L in front of the one you like least (dislike most).
(d) Write NL in front of the one you like next least.

QUESTIONNAIRE 1D

To the Pupil: No.............

Please fill in the spaces below.

Boy or Girl......... Age last birthday......... Grade in school.........

Directions

Suppose you are required to write something about movies—silent films, "talkies," actors or actresses, news films, or anything else connected with the movies. In which of the following ways would you prefer to write? The title must have something to do with the movies, but if you would like to write in some particular way suggested below on a topic about the movies different from the one suggested, that would be satisfactory. Read the entire list through carefully before you decide. Then do what the directions at the bottom of the page tell you to do.

6. Write a letter inquiring about some topic such as: the cost of a movie machine suitable for your school, the cost of a portable movie kodak, or securing some films for use in your school.
7. Write a poem about something connected with movies or movie characters.
8. Write a news article suitable for a school newspaper about some good movie to see, some new movie invention, or the like.
9. Write an editorial suitable for a school newspaper on some such topic as: The Value of Movies for Recreation, or Movies Suitable for School Assemblies.
10. Write an argument for or against some topic concerned with the movies, such as: Sound Pictures are Superior to Silent Pictures, or Movies in School Help Us to Learn.
1. Make up a story about or for the movies.
2. Describe your favorite movie character, or the interior of some new movie theatre, or something similar.
3. Explain some operation about movies, such as: filming a movie, how sound pictures are produced, or how news reel photographers do their work.
4. Give reasons why you like or dislike something about the movies, such as: some movie character, "talkies," or taking your own moving pictures.
5. Write a letter to a friend telling about some movie film or character you have seen recently.

(a) Write a B in front of the one you like best.
(b) Write NB in front of the one you like next best.
(c) Write L in front of the one you like least (dislike most).
(d) Write NL in front of the one you like next least.

APPENDIX IV

UNCLASSIFIED FREE CHOICE COMPOSITION TITLES

SEVENTH GRADE

Boys	Girls
A Dizzy Game	A Child Visits a Doctor
A Trip	An Easter Present
The Chestnut Grove	My Trip to Mars
The Story of the Navy	Thanksgiving
The Catfish	The Beloved Rogue
Bob Hunt at the Senior Camp	Gangler's Circus
I Am Interested in a New Bank	Falling Asleep on a Train
Cartoons	Miss What's Boarding House
A Dictionary	Sleep
The Ohio Flood of 1913	Fun of the Eskimo Children
My Father's Tire Store	An Interview with Musical Mike
Playing Caddy	The World Book
Hanging a Picture	How to Carry On a Business Meeting
My Visit on a Battleship	
Mineola Fair	

EIGHTH GRADE

Boys	Girls
The Clock	Why I Like My Friends
The Molding of a Man	Happy Hours at Work and Play
The Next World War	Routine
The Next War	Why I'm Glad I Am a Girl
The Car I Like Best	My Walk to School on a Country Road in the Springtime
An Imaginary Experience	
How Boat-Making Grew	Why I Would Like to Have a Home of My Own
My Floating Air Castle	
How Things Work	The Orphans' Home
An Obsolete Weapon	Our College Heroes
Autumn in New York	Being a Girl
Woods	A School Day in Norway
My Hero	Thanksgiving Day
Why Johnny Likes Spring	Brush
The Danger of Carrying Matches in Your Pocket	A Story Made Up of Titles of Books
	My Imaginary Tree House
Dr. Cobb's Mummies	The Way I'd Like to Live
Studying People—in Society	April Fools' Day

Boys	Girls
Girls as a Pest	The First of April
The Glory of the Submarine	A Wedding
The Thanksgiving Coming	
A Fish Story	

NINTH GRADE

Boys	Girls
Television	A Substitute for Rubber
Kalamazoo, Michigan	How to Get a Book at the Library
My Friend Goes to Detroit	Uses of Petroleum
The National Forest System	How to Care for Babies
A Short History of Fire Instruments	The Chrysler Building
A Job That Keeps You Busy	Why Some People Think the World Is Going to the Dogs
Our Experience with a Ford	The Writing of a Story
Why I Would Like to Join the Army	Why I Respect Persons Who Have Become Famous
How Will We Cross the Atlantic in the Future?	Finch
The Life of American Indians	"J. C."
How an Operation for Appendicitis Is Made	Lieutenant Garyson
An Old Horn	I, as a Well-Trained Ford
My Pal	A Description of Bear Cave
Hobo Jack	Eskimos
Oil	The Ancients Were Not So Green
Uses of Libraries	The Battle with the Clever Bug That Eats Houses
The Indians	The Whale and the Fish
The Jungle	The Old and Modern Blue Monday
The First English Theatre	Study of Textiles
What To Do in Case of Fire	Jack's Den as an Interesting Room
Labor	Imagination
Artesian Wells	Silvertone
After School	The Red Child of the Forest
On a Moonlit Creek	Our New Neighbors
We're in the Army Now, etc.	The Garden of a Roman Villa
A Poem	The Indians
How to Get $3.75 for Rabbit Meat	Styles
On the Road to the Poorhouse	My Hero
Telephone Conversation	The Story of Radio
Harold Stonerock	A Lost Child
Radio	Armistice Day
Eskimos	A Fight for the Girls of Today
	Back Stage

TENTH GRADE

Boys	Girls
A Visit to the Dentist	How We Spent the First Night of the Snowstorm
The Story of the Three Sons	Heritage Is Doomful
His Last Deed	Her Life Among the Indians
Why the U. S. A. is a Strong and Prosperous Nation	Hercuneen Beloved
A Gang War	Description
How Tubby Broke His Leg	New Spring Clothes
Working	A Shopping Trip
Progress Tomorrow	A Harbor
A Truck Stuck in the Mud	Advertising as News
The Story of a Ship	Just People
Forest Conservation	Silos
Automobile Racing	The History of Matches
In Case of Fire	War and Peace
Various Fighting Implements of the Army Air Corps	Newspapers
	Kalamazoo
Real Life of a Cowboy	Modern Youth
Radio Progress	Hotels
The Uncertain World	4,000 Years from Now
Nothing—My Favorite Theme	Autobiography of a Penny
Life in the Arctic	What a Foreigner Feels Like in America
Fire Prevention	I Do Not Like to Write
The Modern Dog Hospital	Pen Pals
Fires	Art of Acting
The Christmas Seal Sale	Early Shopping
Tobacco	A View from My Window
The Christmas Rush	Thrift
Life of African Savages	When the Snake Goes Easter Shopping
The Future of the U. S. Navy	The Forest
Window Shopping	Midnight Moving
A Club	A White Greenhouse
California Fruit	The Burning of Crystal Palace
Christmas Seals	Students' Stupidity
Why We Should Praise Policemen	Friends
Kalamazoo	A Small Town
Yesterday and Today	Imagination
How Kalamazoo Has Changed	Expressions
The Educational Value of the Postage Stamp	What We Think of a Dentist Behind His Back
Thrift	The Beauty of Words and Sincere Friendship
Early Morning on the Milk Route	My Life as a Pencil
American Citizenship	
The Future of America Depends on the Boys and Girls of Today	Advantages Boys and Girls Should Have in Modern Life

Appendix

Boys	Girls
The Bureau of Engraving and Printing	
The Dangers of Living in the City	
Michigan as a National Playground	
Truth About Fiction	
The Beauty of Work	
Drafting Standards	
How Automobiles Affect the World	
Ad Men Get a Mad-On	
Beating Paul Whiteman at His Own Game	
The Ways of the World	
My Opinion of German Submarine Commanders	

ELEVENTH GRADE

Boys	Girls
Development of Transportation	The Value of Advertising
The Value of Instruments	The Quest for Beauty
A Spectator at a College Football Game	Romance of the Olden Days
	Huntington
A Sunset	Dreams
A Wine Farmer	A Buck Deer of Stamford
Collecting Money	Dreams That Won't Come True
The Army Drill	The Life History of a Stick of Gum
The Reading Room of the Ferguson Library	A Soldier's Dictionary of the Trenches
	The Walking Pair
"Une Thème"	Detectives and Detective Stories
Automobile Racing	A Rolling Stone (poem)
The U. S. Merchant Marine	An Original Composition
Silence	News Office on Monday Morning
Transportation	Why Some People Get Stage Fright
The Five and Ten on the Day of a Sale	Modern Girls Are Just as Good as the Old-Fashioned Ones
The Miracle of Child Genius	
Punch and Oberon (original poem)	
America's Wonders of the World	
The Posterity of America	
Mars of the Future	
American Scenery	

TWELFTH GRADE

Boys	Girls
Random Thoughts	City Homes in Summer
Indigo	What is Life?
This Question of Clothing—A Discussion of Style	The Frivolities of Youth
Solitude	

APPENDIX V

UNCLASSIFIED REASONS WHICH PUPILS GAVE FOR CHOOSING SPECIFIC TOPICS

SEVENTH GRADE

Boys

Because:

1. It is not safe to feed tramps.
2. It is partly true.
3. My father is sick and hasn't had work since the middle of the summer.
4. If I had a million dollars you might know what I would do with it.
5. If I had a million dollars I would know what I would do with it.
6. I could do many things with so much money.
7. If I ever get a million dollars I would know what to do with it.
8. I think I'll have to have one (vocation) sometime.
9. It is necessary in life to know.
10. An animal seems like a person.
11. It was true.
12. It is the largest Zeppelin in the world.
13. Hoover is a very important man.
14. There is good literature in these books I wrote of.
15. I was interested to see how much of a good book I remember.

Girls

Because:

1. It is something everybody has to look forward to.
2. I earn it [spending money] honestly.
3. I think there is enough in that group of words to give a good "imagination" of what would happen.
4. It is a case where you use your imagination which I can do.
5. I wanted to.
6. I wanted to.
7. I thought there wouldn't be very many writing on it.
8. He is President of the United States.
9. So I will be better in school.
10. I'm not in the habit of having a day I will never forget.

EIGHTH GRADE

BOYS

Because:
1. I am old enough to earn my own money.
2. If people read my composition they may be saved from sickness or robbery if they do not feed tramps.
3. It makes you guess who and what the tyrant is.
4. It may be a lesson to someone else never to feed tramps.
5. I like a story that happens out in the open.
6. Some other child might be able to work like me also.
7. Such a thought would never come true.
8. It is the most sensible of all the titles.
9. Of what the title means.
10. I like to know more about old cars.
11. The reason is true.
12. I like to keep my ambition so if I see anything else I like I won't fall for it.

GIRLS

Because:
1. I had to use my imagination.
2. I thought it was interesting to express my thoughts in other words.
3. I am interested in George Washington because I am a descendant of him.
4. I never took a big trip like that.
5. It is true.
6. I took one [trip].
7. I would like to see what I would do with a million dollars.
8. I would like to have everything done for me.
9. I think it will help me to realize my ambition for teaching.
10. I should like to see so many things done with a million dollars.
11. So many quit school when passed from the eighth grade.
12. I want to get a job this summer.
13. If somebody goes in to cheer invalids up or take flowers it helps out a lot.
14. I realize how much my parents do for me and I would like to help them in return.
15. I wanted to see what I would write on this subject.
16. I would do that if I had a million dollars.
17. It is true.
18. I don't like spooky things.

NINTH GRADE

BOYS

Because:
1. It shows the progress from when baseball started until now.
2. It proves that all games are not meant for children.
3. It offers a good field for writing on an imaginary subject.

114 *Written Composition Interests of High School Pupils*

Boys

Because:
4. It was a subject that would be useful to any person that reads it.
5. I like to arouse the peoples' interest when they read the story.
6. It is true.
7. It gives me the idea how the automobiles are progressing from the 19th century to the 20th century.
8. It may help other people.
9. It impressed me most.
10. You can't go through the world without sportsmanship.
11. It gives examples to other boys.
12. You get a lot of experience from traveling.
13. Its lessons are being taught everywhere.
14. It just happened to come to my mind.
15. If anyone wanted to know how I earned my living they could look it up.
16. It is something I should be thinking of.
17. I should know what the greatest American sport is.
18. Helping mother and father is most useful.
19. It is part of our life.
20. It means a great deal to a boy who has played in a game.
21. It builds up your body by playing on a team.
22. You learn self-control.
23. You should grow physically as well as mentally.
24. It is a summary of my later life and would help me get a job.
25. It is the best place of any for a person to go.

Girls

Because:
1. To let others know how to earn spending money.
2. It always holds true in everything.
3. It is one of the most helpful things to humanity.
4. Sometime it might save a good many minutes and dollars.
5. I have always wondered about the right kind of chum.
6. You can get a better idea of what you would do with a large sum of money.
7. Learns a lesson to be thrifty if one earns his own money.
8. Hoover is our President.
9. I feel queer when my compositions are read in class and I should like to get over this.
10. It would be interesting to see which movie I like best.
11. It is better to write on a subject that is worth while than wasting your time.
12. Amusing myself is one of my greatest problems.
13. It tells of other people's experiences and we are warned of the pitfalls of other people.
14. I do not know why I like it.
15. Anything that has happened to me is more easily written about.
16. A certain feeling creeps over me when my themes are read in class.

Appendix

GIRLS

Because:
17. We have to obey good sportsmanship.
18. I have never written on anything like it before.
19. It is interesting to know what the products of our city are.
20. Applies to all games—tells if you are stubborn.
21. Hard problem and takes a lot of thought.
22. I never have found the right kind of chum.
23. I think it gives a person a help in his education to travel.
24. I cannot walk or sit without feeling the effect of what I am writing about.
25. The title attracts attention.
26. This musical instrument is becoming popular.
27. You can make it up.
28. It is a good thing to make a specific example of.

TENTH GRADE

BOYS

Because:
1. There are so many bad bargains going on today.
2. My aunt is all the time telling me what they will do to a person.
3. One can put it into many forms.
4. It is rather hard to earn a school letter or emblem.
5. Pictures in the paper of New York skyscrapers made me think of the new buildings here.
6. Baseball will soon be here and it seems good to think of it.
7. I wanted to find out just what I would do with a million dollars.
8. I think a dog is like a human being.
9. It was the first incident that came to my mind.
10. I thought of the different things I could do with a million dollars.
11. Many people learn lessons by it.
12. Everyone must give some thought to what he is going to do in life.
13. It is the most important thing in my mind.
14. It would give others an idea how to earn money.
15. It is true.

GIRLS

Because:
1. Some people don't know why students quit school.
2. Health is a necessity.
3. I think it will help me if I write and think about it.
4. It is some place you go regularly.
5. This topic is probably the most discussed by parents about the time summer vacation begins.
6. I expect to earn my living.
7. I expect to earn my living.
8. It will be my first problem after I graduate.

GIRLS

Because:
9. I wished others to be interested in skating.
10. I never had a million dollars and never will.
11. Very suggestive—excites the imagination.
12. There are people like that in the world.
13. The title is different.
14. It makes a difference who you choose for a chum.
15. It appeals to the imagination.
16. Girls are of different types and I would like to know which one I really care for.
17. It is true.
18. My thoughts about this title were amusing.
19. It is a good topic to use your imagination.
20. It gave a chance for good fiction.

ELEVENTH GRADE

BOYS

Because:
1. This subject includes many phases of life.
2. I believe dirigibles will be the most important phase in aviation.
3. I wanted to see what I woul. say on the subject.
4. I was interested in the results of his flights on the nation.
5. Education is needed for particular work and much should be considered in choosing work.
6. It is the most important on the list.
7. Lindbergh has done a great deal for peace.
8. Of the importance of automobiles in everyday life.
9. Henry Ford has done much to lower prices of cars so poor men can have them.
10. Players who get on teams get through school easier.
11. Many pupils quit school for some reason.
12. I never saw or heard it discussed before.
13. Babe Ruth is in the limelight.

GIRLS

Because:
1. Tom Sawyer was a regular boy.
2. It appeals to my mood and thought.
3. I want the older generation to know the ideas of the younger.
4. It broadens your knowledge of the country.
5. I want people to realize what it means to be a sick person.
6. It is hard to get a chum you really like.
7. By telling how we work in class it might help others out in their classes.
8. I feel funny having my themes read aloud.
9. It will help me to remember.

GIRLS

Because:
10. People who have quit school have almost quit living.
11. There is a lot of good done in taking trips.
12. I never could have thought of such a title.
13. Of the enormous amount of students who quit school.
14. I can use my imagination and it takes no knowledge which I do not possess.
15. This topic will help me in my profession after I leave school.
16. Good health is most essential.
17. There are many things I can do for my mother.
18. Flowers are appreciated by the sick.
19. Your life is judged by the chums you have.
20. It helps me to think.
21. I am one of a family of moderate means and do not have much money with which to do as I want.
22. It gave me a thought to see what I would do.
23. Something happened to our family and I thought it'd clear up the subject for some people.
24. It taught me a lesson.
25. The topic is diffcrent than ordinary.

TWELFTH GRADE

BOYS

Because:
1. The automobile is an important factor in our lives.
2. I never thought much and I hope this will arouse my interest.

GIRLS

Because:
1. I wished to explain some of the uses electric appliances can be.